who
killed
change?

Also by Ken Blanchard

THE ONE MINUTE ENTREPRENEUR *(with Don Hutson)*, 2008

LEADING AT A HIGHER LEVEL *(with the Founding Associates and Consulting Partners of The Ken Blanchard Companies)*, 2007

SELF LEADERSHIP AND THE ONE MINUTE MANAGER *(with Susan Fowler and Laurence Hawkins)*, 2005

THE LEADERSHIP PILL *(with Marc Muchnick)*, 2003

FULL STEAM AHEAD! *(with Jesse Stoner)*, 2003

THE SERVANT LEADER *(with Phil Hodges)*, 2003

THE ONE MINUTE APOLOGY *(with Margret McBride)*, 2003

ZAP THE GAPS! *(with Dana Robinson and Jim Robinson)*, 2002

WHALE DONE! *(with Thad Lacinak, Chuck Tompkins and Jim Ballard)*, 2002

HIGH FIVE! *(with Sheldon Bowles, Donald Carew and Eunice Parisi-Carew)*, 2000

MANAGEMENT OF ORGANIZATIONAL BEHAVIOR *(with Paul Hersey)*, 8th edition, 2000

BIG BUCKS! *(with Sheldon Bowles)*, 2000

LEADERSHIP BY THE BOOK *(with Bill Hybels and Phil Hodges)*, 1999

THE HEART OF A LEADER, 1999

GUNG HO! *(with Sheldon Bowles)*, 1998

MANAGING BY VALUES *(with Michael O'Connor)*, 1997

MISSION POSSIBLE *(with Terry Waghorn)*, 1996

EMPOWERMENT TAKES MORE THAN A MINUTE *(with John P. Carlos and Alan Randolph)*, 1996

EVERYONE'S A COACH *(with Don Shula)*, 1995

RAVING FANS *(with Sheldon Bowles)*, 1993

THE ONE MINUTE MANAGER BUILDS HIGH PERFORMING TEAMS *(with Don Carew and Eunice Parisi-Carew)*, 1990

THE ONE MINUTE MANAGER MEETS THE MONKEY *(with William Oncken, Jr., and Hal Burrows)*, 1989

THE POWER OF ETHICAL MANAGEMENT *(with Norman Vincent Peale)*, 1988

THE ONE MINUTE MANAGER GETS FIT *(with D. W. Edington and Marjorie Blanchard)*, 1986

LEADERSHIP AND THE ONE MINUTE MANAGER *(with Patricia Zigarmi and Drea Zigarmi)*, 1985

PUTTING THE ONE MINUTE MANAGER TO WORK *(with Robert Lorber)*, 1984

THE ONE MINUTE MANAGER *(with Spencer Johnson)*, 1982

KEN BLANCHARD

bestselling author of *The One Minute Manager*

who killed change?

solving the
mystery of leading people
through change

with **JOHN BRITT PAT ZIGARMI JUDD HOEKSTRA**

HarperCollinsPublishers

HarperCollins*Publishers*
77–85 Fulham Palace Road,
Hammersmith, London W6 8JB

www.harpercollins.co.uk

First published by HarperCollins*Publishers* 2008

1 3 5 7 9 10 8 6 4 2

© Polvera Publishing and John Britt 2009

A catalogue record of this book is
available from the British Library

ISBN 978-0-00-731749-3

FSC is a non-profit international organisation established to promote the
responsible management of the world's forests. Products carrying the FSC
label are independently certified to assure consumers that they come
from forests that are managed to meet the social, economic and
ecological needs of present and future generations.

Find out more about HarperCollins and the environment at
www.harpercollins.co.uk/green

In loving memory of
Alice Britt Caldwell
1943–2007
and
Gerald A. Embry
1941–2008

Contents

who killed change?

Scene of the Crime

AGENT Mike McNally's dark sedan skidded up to the front door of the ACME organization under a stormy night sky. The single blue light rotating on the hood contrasted eerily with the distant flashes of lightning. McNally got out of his car, brushed the ashes from his overcoat and took a last drag on his cheap cigar.

This was his third homicide case this month, all with the same last name—Change. In fact, the investigation of Change fatalities had become his life's work. A clear pattern to the deaths had emerged over the years. Change would be introduced to an organization with varying degrees of reception. From all appearances Change would begin to integrate into the organization and then, without warning, Change would be found dead, quite often with no apparent injury. The evidence was always scant and a sole perpetrator had never been identified.

This time McNally was determined to catch the killer. He extinguished his cigar, took his notebook from his pocket and slowly walked toward the door.

McNally slipped under the yellow Do Not Cross police tape and walked into the conference room. The room buzzed with activity. A photographer was taking pictures of the deceased from different angles, and people in groups of two and three were giving their opinions on what had happened. At the far end of the room, Change's body was slumped over the conference table. Just out of reach of his right hand was an overturned glass. The table was still wet from the spill.

A man unknown to McNally came up to him and handed him a folded note. "The medical examiner asked me to give this to you," he said.

McNally unfolded the note and read:

- probably a homicide
- poisoning is the most likely cause of death
- death was most likely between 7 and 9 A.M. today
- more after the autopsy

McNally cleared the room, closed the door and began his investigation of the crime scene. When he emerged an hour later, a woman was waiting for him outside the door.

"My name is Anna," she said. "I'll be your assistant. I've been told to take care of whatever you need."

McNally knew who the primary suspects were. He had done this many times before. The usual suspects were always the same. He opened his notebook and looked at the list he'd prepared:

1. **Culture**—defines the predominant attitudes, beliefs and behavior patterns that characterize the organization
2. **Commitment**—builds a person's motivation and confidence to engage in the new behaviors required by the Change
3. **Sponsorship**—a senior leader who has the formal authority to deploy resources (e.g., time, money and people) toward the initiation, implementation and sustainability of the Change; ultimately responsible for the success of the Change
4. **Change Leadership Team**—actively leads the Change into the organization by speaking with one voice and resolving the concerns of those being asked to change
5. **Communication**—creates opportunities for dialogue with change leaders and those being asked to change
6. **Urgency**—explains why the Change is needed and how quickly people must change the way they work

7. **Vision**—paints a clear and compelling picture of the future after Change has been integrated successfully
8. **Plan**—clarifies the priority of the Change relative to other initiatives and responsibilities; works with those being asked to change to develop a detailed and realistic implementation plan, then to define and build the infrastructure needed to support the Change
9. **Budget**—analyzes proposed Changes from a financial perspective to determine how best to allocate limited resources and ensure a healthy return on investment (ROI)
10. **Trainer**—provides learning experiences to ensure those being asked to change have the skills needed to follow through with the Change and succeed in the future organization
11. **Incentive**—recognizes and/or rewards people to reinforce desired behaviors and results that enable Change
12. **Performance Management**—sets goals and expectations regarding behaviors and results that enable Change, tracks progress toward the goals and expectations, provides feedback and training and formally documents actual results versus desired results

13. **Accountability**—follows through with people to ensure their behaviors and results are in line with agreed upon goals and expectations and that leaders are walking the talk, and institutes consequences when behaviors or results are inconsistent with those that enable Change

McNally tore the sheet of paper from his notebook and handed it to Anna. "I need to interview these people as soon as possible," he said. "I'm thinking thirty to forty-five minutes per person. Can you arrange that?"

"I'll get right on it," she said.

"Also, it would be great if you could get me a copy of the org chart, so I can see who works for whom," McNally added.

The assistant had anticipated this request. She handed McNally a copy of the organizational chart. Then she was gone.

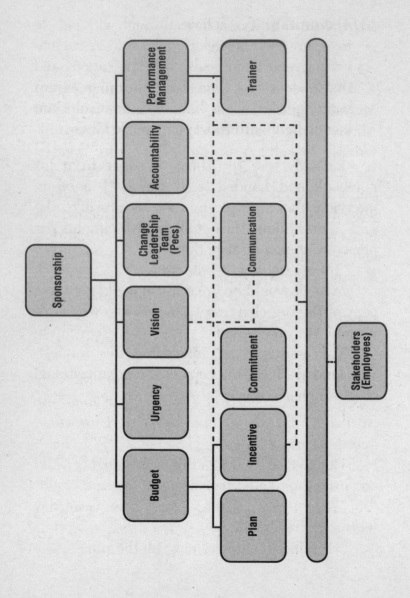

Suspect #1: Culture

AT nine o'clock the next morning Agent McNally, sitting in the same conference room where Change had been killed, read through his file. He looked up as Carolina Culture entered the room. He knew she'd be his first interview but he would never have recognized her. Culture was small and unassuming, neither attractive nor unattractive. She had no distinguishing features, and he thought that if he passed her on the street, he probably wouldn't notice her.

"Good morning," said McNally, trying to hide his surprise. "How are you today?"

"Very well," Culture responded. "And you?" Her voice was smooth and low.

"Good, good. Thank you very much." McNally was thinking, *Why am I asking her how she is? I don't ask people how they are. I ask them questions about the crime.*

Her voice pulled him from his thoughts. "Did you have some questions for me?" she said.

"Yes, I do. Where were you yesterday morning?" he asked.

"I was here. I'm here most all the time."

McNally did not interpret her comment as either whining or martyrdom. It came across as just matter-of-fact. "Did you visit any departments?" he asked.

"Oh, yes. I make my rounds. I'm in every department most every day."

"Did anyone see you up here yesterday?"

"That's an interesting question," Culture replied. "People here are really busy. And let's face it—my role isn't exactly high profile. So I really can't answer that. You'll have to ask them."

McNally found himself straining to hear her. "How would you describe your relationship with Change?" he inquired.

Culture did not hesitate. "Discreet," she offered.

McNally prodded, "Can you help me with that?"

"Change's role is designed to be high profile," she replied. "He consulted me a few times but, in general, it was behind closed doors."

McNally replied, "He consulted you? Were you able to help him?"

"I think so. It's hard to say. It's not my style to micromanage. Since he never discussed any problem with me twice, I assumed he was able to work through the challenges he was facing," she said.

"Micromanage—does that mean Change reported to you?"

"Oh, no," Culture said. McNally thought he noticed a hint of a smile. "No one reports to me. I've been around here longer than you would believe. My role has always been to define the beliefs that guide how we operate here. You could think of my role as a compass that points in a direction, but it's not a map that details how to get from point A to point B."

"So, what was it that Change consulted you about last?" McNally asked.

"VALUES!" Culture replied so loudly that McNally found himself backing up in his chair. She continued at a volume that was much too loud for the size of the room and their proximity to each other. "Change wanted to use our organizational values to leverage what he was trying to get accomplished. I tried to teach him that if your actions are consistent with your values, you have a better chance of success."

"And those values are . . . ?" McNally asked in a soft voice that was perhaps an unconscious attempt to normalize her previous intensity. It didn't work. Culture launched into an even louder monologue that McNally could describe only as overly rehearsed.

"*V* is for Very Efficient. To reach our business goals, we must operate in a manner that is very efficient. We have to appropriately allocate resources and control our costs.

"*A* is for A Customer Focus. We have many customers and we have to provide each of them with the highest level of service.

"*L* is for Lots of Teamwork. We can achieve more by working as a team. At ACME we believe 'no one of us is as smart as all of us!'

"*U* is for Understanding. At the core of understanding is listening. Each individual will bring a point of view to a situation or opportunity. By listening and understanding all points of view, we will make better decisions.

"*E* is for Excellence. Our products are our livelihood. Anything less than excellent is unacceptable."

The contrast between his first impression of Culture and the strength of her presentation about ACME's values was stark. But then McNally considered that strength and decibel level were not necessarily synonymous. He detected no passion in her delivery and sensed that the volume was a substitute for real feeling.

"The values you speak of come through loud and clear," McNally said. "But I'm betting there's a disconnect between those values and what's actually going on here."

Culture did not respond. McNally made a mental note that he had not seen Culture blink the whole time they had been talking.

"Would you mind responding to that?" McNally asked politely.

"Sure—but I didn't perceive it to be a question," she said, lowering her voice. "As I told you before, my job is to lay the groundwork and to point in a direction. I don't control whether the individuals or teams live by our values."

McNally wondered how well Culture knew Accountability. He knew that if Accountability were doing his job well, he would reinforce the behaviors that drive Culture. McNally had worked enough cases to know that there was always some gap between espoused values and the day-to-day behaviors of people in that organization. At this place, he suspected it was more of a wide gulf than a small gap. Surmising that Culture was not going to take any responsibility for the disparity, McNally changed tactics.

"Any idea who killed Change?" he asked.

"Not a clue," Culture responded immediately.

"But surely," McNally coaxed, "with your long history here and the long hours you put in and with your obvious influence on the organization, you must have some idea of who didn't like Change—someone who wanted to get Change out of the way."

"You flatter me, Agent McNally. Yes, I've been around a long time and I do work a lot of hours. I would like to think that I have had, and still have, some influence on this organization. But I still can't tell you who killed Change."

Again McNally found himself leaning forward, mesmerized by the honeyed tone of Culture's voice.

There was a long pause. Then Culture asked, "Anything else?"

"No, I think that's about it. Where can I find you if I have more questions?" he asked.

"Oh, I'll be around," she said.

Again McNally thought he caught a glimpse of a smile. He looked down to consult his notes to see who was next on the list. He looked up and began, "Thank you for your—"

But Culture was gone. He looked behind him and the door was closed. He had not heard it open or shut. With some embarrassment, he actually pulled his chair back and looked under the conference table. Nothing. No one was there.

That's just downright eerie, he thought. *Just downright eerie.*

Suspect #2: Commitment

CHASE Commitment was the next to appear in the interrogation room. With an earnest face, Commitment smiled at Agent McNally, shook his hand and sat down.

McNally opened with "Thank you for meeting me. As you know, I am investigating Change's death. Would you mind telling me a little about yourself?"

"My pleasure," replied Commitment. "Certainly, like most people here, I wear several hats. My main focus, however, is to create buy-in for the Changes we employ here." He stopped and eagerly looked at McNally.

"So tell me more. Can you tell me how you work with leadership here in regard to Change?"

"Happy to," answered Commitment with a smile. "I'm not sure who you have interviewed so far and I wouldn't want to 'steal their thunder,' as they say. I can tell you that I have learned a lot from the Changes we've had here over the years. The greatest lesson I've learned is that our employees have fairly predictable concerns when we introduce a new Change. If we don't respond to those concerns, the success of Change drops dramatically. When Change is first introduced, everybody seems to need more information. They want to hear why they need Change. I work with Ernest Urgency on that. They also have personal concerns—who wouldn't wonder if they'll win or lose when someone announces a Change? Whether leadership likes it or not, employees don't buy in to a Change until they understand how it might affect them. Don't you see, Agent McNally, that if we get at these concerns and address them, we are more likely to gain employee support? Again, that's my job."

McNally felt Commitment's passion. In fact, he could envision Commitment on stage behind a podium delivering a motivation speech, his audience in reverent attention.

Commitment continued, "We must be able to create a picture of the Change and help our people see what it will look like. I need Victoria Vision for that. And doesn't it make sense that we should let some of our people be involved in the decision making about Change? I lean on Spence Sponsorship and Pecs for that."

"Pecs?" McNally asked.

"You'll meet him later, I'm sure. Everybody knows Pecs. Anyway, after Change has been here a while, our employees wonder whether or not Change can really be integrated. Perry Plan should be involved. Terry Trainer should be doing some training, and Isabella Incentive should provide the encouragement."

Commitment stood up and began pacing, palms and eyes raised to the ceiling as if speaking to a higher authority. "Eventually, employees have concerns about whether everyone will be able to truly work together. It's here that I need you more than ever, Peter Performance Management and Aidan Accountability."

McNally found himself looking around to see if someone had entered the room. Nobody had.

Head and hands down now, Commitment walked back to his chair and sat down. McNally noticed that the suspect was sweating profusely. He grabbed a bottle of water and placed it in front of Commitment.

"Wow, as I was listening to you just now, I felt as though I was listening to a sermon," McNally replied. "But despite all your passion, I couldn't help thinking that your colleagues might not be totally on board with the lessons you have learned about Change."

Commitment's expression told McNally that he was having an internal debate as to how much information he wanted to share. Finally, Commitment said, "We're a bit dysfunctional here."

McNally used silence to urge Commitment to continue.

"It's funny you said 'sermon' earlier," Commitment continued at last, "because that pretty much sums up what I feel like I'm doing here—preaching. The congregation—made up of leaders and managers—comes every Sunday. They smile, nod, shake my hand and then go out and behave any way they want Monday through Saturday. Academically, they understand that people are much more likely to buy in to a Change when they are involved in the planning and have an opportunity to influence decisions. The leaders and managers are just not, may I say, committed to consistently applying the knowledge. And they fool themselves into thinking our employees don't see what's going on."

Commitment looked exhausted. This was odd, considering that McNally had heard Commitment was typically full of energy and enthusiasm. "One more question," McNally said. "Do you know who might have killed Change?"

"I truly don't," replied Commitment earnestly. "It's hard for me to believe that people wouldn't be committed to Change given what he was trying to do."

Once again they shook hands, and Commitment left the room.

Reflections on Culture and Commitment

T AKING a break from the interviews, McNally stepped outside the office, lit a cigar and thought about what he had learned from Culture and Commitment. He wrote in his notebook some ideas about what he'd learned.

CULTURE

While Culture could readily recite the formal organizational values that were displayed on posters throughout the organization, she wasn't really in tune:

- She did not understand the real values of the organization—the predominant attitudes, beliefs and behavior patterns that characterized the organization.

- When there is a disconnect between stated values and the way an organization actually operates, the values posted on the wall are disregarded. Employees become skeptical, even cynical, about leaders who say one thing and do another. The real culture and values always speak louder than the stated ones. Change would have been better off spending his time trying to understand and align himself with the real culture and values of ACME than seeking advice from Culture.

COMMITMENT

Commitment is an interesting character:

- He knows that people are more likely to buy in to a decision that they've influenced than a decision imposed on them by others. He also knows that uncovering the predictable concerns people have in the face of Change allows the concerns to be addressed, increasing both trust and buy-in.

- Despite his passion, Commitment was not able to convince the leaders of the organization to act on his knowledge. As a result, the people left out of influencing Change reminded the leaders that they could derail or even kill him.

Were Culture and Commitment viable suspects? At this point in the investigation, McNally didn't know. He had more questions than answers.

- Did Change understand Culture well enough to align with her or try to change her?
- Did the senior leaders understand that while it is true that decisions can be made faster when fewer people are involved, such decisions do not usually translate into faster, better or more sustainable integration of Change because there's no Commitment without involvement?
- Did those leaders who knew a lot about Culture and Commitment do everything they could to help Change become a real part of the organization?

Suspect #3: Sponsorship

SPENCE Sponsorship was a walking advertisement in a men's fashion magazine. From his shined shoes to his perfect hair, he hadn't missed a single detail. Agent McNally glanced at his own wrinkled shirt, loosened tie and dull black shoes, and made a mental note that he could not allow himself to dislike Sponsorship because of his image. Dispassionately, McNally asked, "So, what do you do here in the organization?"

"One of the main jobs I have," replied Sponsorship, "is to be the executive sponsor of a Change's major effort here and ensure we have a Change Leadership Team that works well together. What I mean is that for Change to have a major success at ACME, there must be one person—someone in an influential position—who takes what I call ownership of the Change. To that end, our organization is structured so that I am the one to whom most departments eventually report. Granted, I have directors and managers who take care of the day-to-day operations. But the staff here is keenly aware of my position. If I endorse, shall we say, a project, staff members know that it's going to happen—one way or another."

McNally took a mental note that in Sponsorship's opening discourse he used the word *I* six times in six sentences. "So how many Change initiatives have you had in the past year?" asked McNally.

Sponsorship did not hesitate. "Four," he said.

With virtually no attempt to mask his sarcasm, McNally asked, "And other than relying on your status and position, what did you actually do that might be perceived as true sponsorship?"

Sponsorship looked puzzled and responded, "I organized meetings and communicated my expectations."

There was a long pause. Finally McNally prompted, "And what else?"

"I have directors and managers to take it from there."

"How well did you know Change?"

"Oh, we were good friends. We played some golf and every once in a while we would get together for a game of racquetball."

"What about your professional relationship?"

"Certainly at these meetings I would put Change front and center. I would leave no doubt in anyone's mind that I was behind Change one hundred percent."

"Then you would let your directors and managers take it from there?" McNally asked.

"Well, yeah. To deal with Change is one of the things I pay them for."

"Let me ask you a question," McNally said. "Married?"

"No."

"All right. Let's say you have a girlfriend who one day tells you she loves you. After that day, you barely talk except when you say hello as you pass in the hall. Is that a relationship you think is going to work out?"

"Well, no, probably not."

"Do you see the connection?" asked McNally.

Sponsorship, looking puzzled, did not respond.

McNally lost his patience. "Look, you cannot expect Change to be successful based on putting him front and center in a few meetings!" Weighing his words carefully, McNally stood up and began pacing the room. "You're overestimating the power of your words. As Sponsorship, you must do more than introduce Change. You must be visible and supportive way beyond the introductory meetings. Your actions are much more powerful than your words. You must remain connected to Change throughout the change process. It's your role to get Aidan Accountability and Isabella Incentive involved. What you reinforce is three times more powerful than what you say. Do you understand?"

McNally looked over at Sponsorship, who seemed mesmerized by his own reflection in the window of the interrogation room.

"Do you understand?" repeated McNally, raising his voice.

Sponsorship turned and looked at him.

"I never thought that much about what I had to do to help Change succeed," he replied with sincerity in his voice. "I guess I thought that because of my position in the organization, I could get people to buy in to Change by just making an announcement."

Spence Sponsorship's comments were interrupted by the ringing of his cell phone. Much to McNally's chagrin, Sponsorship took the call and left the conference room.

McNally sighed. It had been almost impossible to get on this suspect's calendar and McNally had no idea when he'd see him again.

Suspect #4:
Change Leadership Team

AGENT McNally pulled out his little black notebook and looked at the list. So far he had interviewed Carolina Culture, Chase Commitment and Spence Sponsorship. Next on the list was Chester of the Change Leadership Team.

McNally knew from previous cases that a Change Leadership Team was a key ingredient to integrating Change into the organization. The members of this group were chosen because of their influence in the organization. Quite often, the members of the Change Leadership Team had positional power—that is, their title or position in the organization caused people to pay attention to them, but this was not always the case. A wise leader forming a Change Leadership Team would also include informal leaders from all levels of the organization, people with strong technical or people skills in the area in which Change was going to be introduced. For Change to succeed, lots of voices needed to make the case for Change.

As McNally entered the room, he had no doubt as to who was sitting at the opposite end of the table—in the same place where Change had died. Chester of the Change Leadership Team was massive. His biceps had to be three times the size of a normal man's. Where his shoulders intersected with his head, there was very little evidence of a neck.

Agent McNally introduced himself by first and last name and Mr. Change Leadership Team responded in kind. "Look," he added, "most folks just call me 'Pecs.'" He tightened his pectoral muscles, straining the confines of his pullover shirt. "Feel free to call me 'Pecs' if you like."

McNally was reminded that he really should start making it to the gym as he had resolved to do last New Year's Day.

"Okay, Pecs, how well did you know Change?" McNally inquired.

"Fairly well, I would say," replied Pecs. "Change had been here only five or six months and he needed to be elevated in the organization. He needed to be seen by others as important. So that was my job, you know, to hold Change up."

"Did that get old for you, holding him up like that all the time? That must have been tiring," said McNally.

"That's one way to look at it, I guess. But I really considered it to be a free workout. See these biceps?" said Pecs, flexing them. "I put about two inches on them after Change got here."

McNally noted Pecs's unabashed self-confidence.

"Hey, you mind if I get a bottled water?" Pecs asked as he eyed the small refrigerator in the corner.

"Not at all," said McNally. "We'll send the bill to Budget." They both laughed.

When Pecs got up and walked over to get his water, Agent McNally just about fell out of his chair. From the waist up Pecs could double for a world-class bodybuilder, but below the waist he had—well, what came to McNally's mind were pencil legs. McNally had in his head the image of poodle legs walking around with a pit bull's torso. Pecs got his water and returned to his seat.

This new view of Pecs led McNally to change his original line of questioning. "So your main job was to hold Change up?" he prompted.

"That's right," replied Pecs with what seemed to be a note of pride.

"And who carried him out into the organization?" asked McNally.

"I don't know what you mean."

"It's a simple question. Who carried him out into the organization?"

Pecs looked perplexed and was silent.

McNally knew from experience that it takes a leadership team to carry Change out into the organization if you expect Change to be effective. He recalled an organization he had worked with recently that understood this. They were introducing a Change and had put together a leadership team composed of members who had successfully led Changes in the past. These people had the time needed to lead Change, were highly skilled, communicated well and were diverse enough to avoid groupthink and introduce and integrate Change throughout the organization. In short, they had the talent to carry Change forward.

McNally went on. "It's one thing to hold Change up all day and it is another to carry him out into the organization, to interact with the people who may be affected by him."

"Look," said Pecs with a reddening face, "I pulled my weight when it came to Change."

"From an outsider looking in," McNally retorted, "it looks more like you used Change to benefit your own agenda—to build and flex your own muscles. But you really didn't think about what Change or the organization needed."

McNally continued, "Perhaps my last statement was a bit strong, but if you don't mind me saying so, it's obvious you've worked very hard to build your upper-body strength, and I'm sure to some degree you had Change's and the organization's welfare in mind. But I just can't see how you could consistently carry Change out into the organization without stopping frequently for breaks."

Pecs reluctantly admitted, "You're right. I've been out of balance. But when I look in the mirror, I just see myself from the waist up. If I don't see my flaws, then I don't have to deal with them. I'm not one to blame others. That's truly not my style. Spence Sponsorship talks about putting a team together every time a new Change comes, but somehow the responsibility always seems to come back to me."

This was just what Agent McNally had suspected.

Taking pity on Pecs, McNally said, "It's too late for this Change. He is dead and gone. But another Change will come along and you can start working out your lower body. You can get ready to carry Change throughout the organization rather than just pumping him up a few times and then disappearing. The key is balance—doing some of the heavy lifting at the front end and then continuing to support Change throughout the change process."

Pecs nodded and said, "Thanks." With a note of concern he asked, "Are you charging me?"

"I'm not charging anyone until the investigation is complete."

"Are we done?" asked Pecs.

"For now. You're not planning on going anywhere, are you?"

"Just to the gym," said Pecs with a hint of a smile. "I've got some squats to do."

Suspect #5: Communication

A FEW minutes after Pecs left, Clair Communication knocked lightly on the conference room door and entered the room. McNally stood and said, "Hello, I'm Agent Mike McNally. Thank you for your time."

Communication responded with an almost imperceptible smile and a polite nod of her head. Her black hair was shoulder length and she wore full-framed black glasses.

They settled into their respective chairs and McNally said, "I suppose you know why I've asked to talk with you."

Communication nodded.

"Can you describe your working relationship with Change?" McNally asked.

She responded in a whisper, "You'll have to forgive me, I have laryngitis and—"

McNally interrupted, "Would you prefer to postpone the interview?"

"No, no," she whispered. "It's sort of a chronic condition for me." Communication continued, "Change and I worked together on a few projects. He asked for my help in getting the word out to people who needed to be involved."

"Were you able to help him?" McNally inquired.

Communication cupped her hand to her ear. "I'm sorry, could you repeat the question? The batteries on my hearing aid went dead a while ago and I haven't had time to replace them."

"Were you able to help him?" McNally asked, a little louder.

"Oh, yes. I helped him draft some memos and put some storyboards together. And he invited me to most of his meetings to tell people about his plans."

McNally winced. He had learned over the years that although one of Communication's roles was to talk, the other role was to listen. He knew many in Communication's position who were artful with their words and enjoyed telling others what they knew about Change. But the ones who excelled in promoting Change knew how to listen well too.

In a loud voice, McNally made a sharp transition. "Who do you know that would want to see Change gone?"

"Can't say," she whispered almost inaudibly.

"Can't say, or won't say?" demanded McNally.

Communication opened her small notebook, scribbled a few words and pushed the pad over to McNally. The note read: *Can't say. Voice is gone. Does this sometimes. Sorry. Do not know who might want to kill Change.*

McNally now did the scribbling. He gave the pad back to Communication and she read: *Can you explain to me how you can competently fulfill your role when you can't talk some of the time?*

Clair Communication looked up at McNally, forced a brief smile and took the pen and pad back. *I have a staff person that helps me,* she wrote.

McNally sighed. "Please tell me more about this person," he said. "What does he or she do?"

She wrote: *His name is Committee. When we have a tough issue to tackle and my laryngitis flares up, Committee will call a group of people together. He leads the discussions at these meetings.*

"Do you find him effective?" McNally asked doubtfully.

She wrote: *He keeps things moving.*

Controlling his exasperation, McNally took a deep breath and responded, "I asked you if he was effective. Keeping things moving is not, in my mind, synonymous with effectiveness."

McNally had worked with Committees before. Most met regularly but lacked concrete Plans and Accountability. Delegation was frequently called upon in these meetings. Follow-up and Consequences were notably absent.

Communication just stared at McNally. She did not reach for the pen.

"All right," said McNally, "you can go. I may need to talk with you again and I might want to speak with Committee too. So stick around."

Reflections on Sponsorship, Change Leadership Team and Communication

AGENT McNally was feeling very disillusioned after interviewing Sponsorship, Change Leadership Team (aka "Pecs") and Communication. In all his years as an agent, McNally had never before witnessed such a widespread failure of leadership.

He'd picked the wrong case to try to quit smoking on. He stepped outside the office, lit a cigar, took a few puffs and thought about what he had learned from the three suspects he'd just interviewed. He captured his learnings in his notebook, hoping that others could use them to avoid making the same mistakes:

SPONSORSHIP

While Sponsorship may have been saying all the right things due to his fondness for hearing himself speak, his failures were many:

- He didn't model the behaviors expected of others. He didn't seem to know that actions speak louder than words.
- He didn't team up with Incentive to recognize and reinforce the desired behaviors among others.
- He didn't team up with Accountability to show the organization that he was serious about this Change.
- He didn't heed the advice from Commitment about securing Change by surfacing and addressing concerns and involving people being asked to change in the decision-making process.
- He didn't select and align a well-qualified Change Leadership Team; instead, he passively assigned the implementation of Change to his direct reports.

Agent McNally considered how often Sponsorship believes Change just needs a good introduction to be successful. But when Sponsorship does not follow through, Change fails. Then again, it's hard to be actively involved in helping Change succeed from the golf course.

CHANGE LEADERSHIP TEAM, AKA "PECS"

McNally reflected on what he had learned about Pecs:

- He missed a golden opportunity to include advocates for Change on the day-to-day leadership team.
- He colluded with Commitment—they both treated those being asked to change as spectators instead of active participants in the change process.
- Like Sponsorship, Change Leadership Team was considered hypocritical, and his behavior provided yet another excuse for people to resist Change.

COMMUNICATION

Communication also had failings:

- She failed to stay in touch with Sponsorship and Change Leadership Team. This led to mixed messages about Change in the organization, which became, in turn, an easy excuse for people to ignore Change.

- She was too focused on getting the word out and not focused enough on creating dialogue to surface and address people's predictable concerns about Change.

Feeling a little nauseated, McNally put out his cigar. Too much nicotine—or not enough leadership? Probably both.

Suspect #6: Urgency

THE interview with Ernest Urgency was scheduled for 3:00 P.M. Urgency sauntered in around 3:15, excused himself to go get a cup of coffee and came back, ready to be questioned, at 3:25 P.M. *Not a good sign,* thought McNally.

"Are you clear on why you are here?" asked McNally, meeting and holding Urgency's gaze.

"Sure, sure. Change was killed last night right here in this conference room. Only the leaders generally have access to this area of the building, so naturally we would be the first suspects."

Urgency had taken his sweet time getting to the meeting and settling in to his chair, but now that he was seated he was fidgety, repeatedly checking his watch and looking at the door.

"You got a plane to catch?" McNally asked with unrepressed sarcasm.

"Look here," replied Urgency with a reddening face. "I'm sorry that Change was killed. Truly sorry, but I've got a lot of things on my plate that I have to take care of. I didn't kill Change. I barely knew the guy. What motive would I have? This interview or whatever you call it is just a waste of my time."

"So noted," said McNally dryly. "So where were you between six A.M. and noon yesterday?"

"But I thought he was killed last night?" Urgency questioned.

"Maybe he was and maybe he wasn't. Just answer the question," said McNally.

"I need to get my calendar," replied Urgency.

"I'll be right here," said McNally as he leaned back in his chair and put his feet up on the conference room table.

When Urgency left the room, McNally closed his eyes and reflected on his past cases. He knew that for Change to survive, leaders must send Change out with Urgency and managers must accept Change with Urgency, and then introduce Change with Urgency to their staffs. Other Changes had come and gone in these organizations, but the ones who were introduced with Urgency were more likely to be successful. When he was at the top of his game, Urgency would do the following:

- He would send clear and consistent messages about who Change is and what they expect from him.
- He would communicate a compelling business case supporting the need for Change.

- He would articulate the crisis or opportunity necessitating Change and communicate it broadly and dramatically.

Hearing Urgency return, McNally opened his eyes and put his feet back on the floor. "I got here right at seven-forty," Urgency said as he consulted the calendar in his hand. "There was a seven-thirty meeting I was a bit late for and then I was pretty much in meetings all day long."

"No breaks between meetings?" questioned McNally.

"Well, yes, some. But I would not have had time to—" He paused. "Look, I didn't do it!" he exclaimed.

"How did you introduce Change to ACME's managers?"

"Let's see. Change started here about six months ago. We brought him in because our competitors were shrinking our market share. We had a few formal meetings. I let the managers know how important I thought Change's role would be, and then, well, the managers sort of took him from there."

"Took him where?" asked McNally.

"Out to the staff," muttered Urgency.

"How do you know Change got out to the staff?"

"Well, I saw Change in the lunchroom with managers and staff on several occasions," Urgency replied defensively.

McNally stood and began pacing. "Look, we both know what's going on here. Change was the new kid on the block and it was your job not only to get him introduced to the organization but also to get him integrated. It was your job to communicate a rational business case for Change in a way that would motivate the managers and staff to see the immediate need for Change and embrace him. Your calendar is so diluted with perfunctory meetings that you've lost your sense of priorities. You're supposed to be Mr. Urgency, but you can't even make it to a meeting on time. You make me sick. Get out of my sight!"

Without a word, Urgency got up and moved toward the door. Just before he closed it, McNally called out, "Don't leave town!"

Suspect #7: Vision

MCNALLY'S next meeting was with another member of the leadership team—Victoria Vision. When Vision came in he could not help noting the irony that she was wearing rose-colored glasses. *Why not?* thought McNally. If Communication had frequent bouts of laryngitis and a hearing aid, why shouldn't Vision have rose-colored glasses?

McNally knew all too well the power of Vision in an organization, especially when it came to Change. Vision's unique role was to pull herself out of the day-to-day operations and see the organization and its performance not as it is today, but as it could or would be tomorrow, next month, next year and so on. This, in fact, was the easy part of her job. The hard part was to get others to catch glimpses, snapshots and movie clips of what she was seeing.

Vision's role, position and status in the organization allowed her to transcend the minutiae of daily operations. McNally knew that most of the members of the organization did not have that luxury. Vision looked up and out while most others looked down and in. For Vision to be successful, she must get others to look up and out, envision the future and then recalibrate their activities to draw them toward that future. The need for this role was intensified whenever Change came on board.

McNally thought, *I doubt this woman is able to inspire others to see what she sees. With those glasses on, she's overly optimistic and probably not in touch with the reality of the organization.*

Vision sat down, pulled off her glasses and began methodically wiping them with a handkerchief. To McNally, Vision appeared relaxed.

"I didn't do it," Vision said calmly.

"Didn't do what?" said McNally.

"I didn't kill Change."

"Do you know who did?"

"We've all been talking, you know. I have my suspicions, but that's all they are—suspicions. I don't have any proof."

"Would you mind sharing your suspicions with me?"

Vision stopped rubbing the lenses of her glasses. She stared directly at McNally and, after a moment, said, "Okay, but you have to keep it between us. I think some of the staff killed Change."

"*Some* of the staff? Not one of the staff?" McNally asked.

"It could have been just one, but I think it was a group."

"A group? What group?"

Before Vision could reply, there was a knock on the door. Anna dropped two menus in front of them and stated, "I know both of you missed lunch. Circle what you want. I'll be back in a few minutes to pick these up."

Both of them obeyed, scanning their respective menus. When McNally finished circling his order, he looked up and noticed that Vision had set aside her rose-colored glasses and put on a pair of glasses with lenses as thick as Coke bottles to read the menu.

The irony is growing by the minute, McNally mused to himself.

Vision completed her task, replaced the Coke-bottle glasses in their case, pocketed the case and resumed polishing her other glasses.

"Where were we?" Vision asked. "Oh, yeah. The group. Can't really say for sure, but if I were an agent working on this case, I might nose around the Purchasing department a bit. You didn't hear that from me, of course."

Agent McNally baited the hook and went fishing. "So if you were an agent working on this case and happened to wander into the Purchasing department, what would be the first question you'd ask?"

"Let's see. First, I'd throw out a couple of innocent questions. Get them comfortable with me. Then I might ask how the new just-in-time inventory process was going."

"I presume it is not going well."

"You are a bright agent," Vision responded.

"When did they go to this new process?"

"Five or six months ago."

"Was this a major transition for them?"

"Oh, definitely. Our inventory was killing us." Vision's face suddenly turned crimson. "Sorry! 'Killing' was probably a poor choice of words."

"How well did the people in the department know Change?"

"I don't think they knew each other well. Acquaintances, I would say. Just acquaintances."

"But isn't that your job? To make sure the employees can picture themselves with Change in the future?"

Vision stared at McNally blankly.

"I mean, you just admitted that this Change was a major transition for that department. If they have been operating under one paradigm for years and suddenly they're informed that they need to do a one-eighty, don't you think their chances of success would be greater if Change were more than a mere acquaintance?"

"So are you trying to say this is my fault?" Vision asked.

"Where were you yesterday morning?" McNally inquired.

Vision now looked nervous. She was doing double-time on her glasses. "From seven to eight I was in a board meeting. We were reviewing the strategic plan draft. After that I did some paperwork in my office until about nine forty-five and then I had to leave for an optometry appointment."

Irony, irony, irony, thought McNally.

Vision went on. "Look, I don't have a motive. Most of my job revolves around three things: paying attention to new trends and technologies, scanning for new ideas and opportunities and creating a picture of the future that's inspiring. I need Change. Why would I want to kill him?"

Maybe she's not as clueless as I thought she was, McNally mused silently. "I'm not accusing you of killing Change," McNally said. *But you didn't prevent him from dying,* he thought. "Even so, I don't want you to go anywhere for a few days."

There was another knock on the door and Anna came back in to pick up the menus. Vision, looking pale, got up and put her glasses back on. "I'm not hungry," she said, and walked out.

Reflections on Urgency and Vision

As McNally sat alone waiting for his lunch to arrive, he thought about what he'd heard and not heard from Urgency and Vision. He was running out of room in his notebook, so he started using the back side of pages as he captured his learnings.

URGENCY

Urgency was a likely suspect based on his inconsistent behavior:

- He tried to get people to accept Change, but he never convinced them that the status quo was no longer a viable option.
- He neglected to spend enough time with those who felt the pain of the status quo.
- He didn't spend enough time with those who saw the opportunity for performance levels to rise with the integration of Change.
- He failed to ask others why they thought the organization needed Change. The case for Change is always more compelling when the people being asked to adopt Change are brought face-to-face with the facts and invited to offer their thoughts.

VISION

Vision was clearly a suspect for the murder of Change:

- She didn't see her own organization clearly.
- She ignored the advice of Commitment. A Vision created during an off-site executive retreat doesn't mean much to someone on the front line who had no say in the vision. The more Vision can get people involved in the visioning process, the more likely it is that they will want to be part of the organization in the future.
- She didn't secure the buy-in she needed to attain her inspiring vision. Most leaders, trying to initiate a Change, announce the Change ("Here's what we're going to do!"), set unclear or confusing expectations ("We're raising the bar!"), send people to training and prematurely celebrate victory. They forget to paint an inspiring post-Change picture of the organization that includes their people in it.

Suspect #8: *Plan*

PERRY Plan was Agent McNally's next interviewee and it irritated McNally that he, like Urgency, was not on time. Plan had called to say he was on his way from the airport and would be there in ten or fifteen minutes.

When Plan did arrive, McNally was surprised to see him clad in a leather jacket with a wings emblem on each sleeve. He plopped a heavy black valise down at his feet.

"You must be Agent McNally." Plan flashed a smile as he reached out to shake McNally's hand. "Sorry I'm late. Yes, sorry I'm late. It's such a beautiful day that I had to take advantage of it. I took off this morning. Not a cloud in the sky. I just got back."

McNally finished the handshake and gestured for Plan to sit. "Thank you for joining me. I assume you know why I have asked to speak with you."

"Yes, yes, I do. Terrible thing, Change's death. A tragedy indeed."

"Let me start, if you don't mind, by asking you what you do here."

Plan fell silent, deep in thought. Finally, McNally cleared his throat and brought Plan back to the present. "Ah, yes. What I do here. What I do here. Hmm, well, one might say my key role here is to prepare ACME for the Changes that are coming."

"Strategic or tactical?" inquired McNally.

"I don't understand the question," replied Plan.

It was Plan's job to know those terms. With a hint of sarcasm, McNally said, "You do know the difference between strategic and tactical, I assume?"

"Certainly I know the difference," answered Plan with subtle defensiveness.

"So when you are preparing ACME for these Changes, are you involved strategically, tactically or both?"

"Oh, I see now," replied Plan as the smile returned to his face. "Strategically, for the most part." He paused and looked thoughtful for a moment. "You know," he resumed, "I think that that is why I enjoy flying so much. Big-picture view, you know. Nothing like it." After a long pause Plan said, "This may sound crazy, but I like all the new proposed Changes. A real challenge to the gray cells." He tapped the side of his head with a finger. "Love to theorize about how the Change could fit in and what the expected outcome will be. I get the same feeling as being in control of a good airplane. Great sensation!"

"But surely you can't take every activity or project associated with a Change up for a ride. You can't reasonably pilot all of them, can you? You must have some sort of screening process, right?"

"Used to," Plan replied. "Had a colleague but she's been on sick leave for a while. Prioritization is her name. Worked in the tower. Traffic control tower, that is. She was quite a stickler for regulations. My philosophy is a bit different from hers and, well, to tell you the truth, I just have trouble saying no. Anyway, it really doesn't take too much of my time and if we employ a Change and it doesn't work out, no harm done, right?"

McNally did not respond.

Plan added with an embarrassed look, "I guess the 'no harm done' part depends on who you ask. I must admit that Bailey Budget stays on my case about the number of projects we take on with each Change."

"You've certainly given me a lot of good information about how you're managing the strategic piece of your job," McNally said. "But you must be spending at least some time and energy on the tactical piece. Otherwise, you could never help Change, may I say, get off the ground."

"Infrastructure's job," replied Plan.

"Infrastructure?" asked McNally.

"Yeah, he's the tactical guy. Not my cup of tea, you might say. He works on the business processes and development of tools to support those business processes for Change, I think."

"You think?" inquired McNally caustically.

"Look," replied Plan, "there's no need to get testy here. I'm just passing on to you what I have been told. I am trying to answer your questions the best way I can. Supposedly, Ira Infrastructure works with Peter Performance Management and Isabella Incentive to make sure the employees have the technology and systems to work with the Change. But you must understand, I spend most of my time in the air so I can see the bigger picture—the strategic view, you might say. Vicki Vision and Spence Sponsorship like to go up with me every now and then. But Infrastructure, he works at ground level. So to be honest, I'm not really sure about what he does. You'll have to ask him."

With unrestrained sarcasm McNally asked, "Do you ever come down out of the clouds long enough to plan the details of how the Change should be implemented?"

Plan took in and let out a long, deep breath to control his impatience. "Again, Agent McNally, I can tell you what I think I know but I can't be in two places at one time. Besides Infrastructure, Measurement has to pay attention to all the details. He has to work with Performance Management and Change to define outcomes for service and quality. Supposedly, Measurement monitors ACME's outcomes against these benchmarks. And before you ask," Plan said with one hand up in a defensive posture, "I have never actually met Measurement. I keep busy, well, planning."

McNally was fed up with this "it's not my department" mentality. "Let me ask you a question," he said. "Since you like to fly so much, who ensures that a flight goes well?" asked McNally.

"I do," replied Plan with a look of confusion on his face. "I'm the pilot."

Plan cocked his head to the side, looking unsure about where McNally was going with this line of questioning.

"I don't fly nearly as often as you do," McNally continued, "but here's what I think I know. To have a successful flight, you need a flight plan. When, where, how, how fast, et cetera, right?"

Plan started to respond but was halted by McNally's upraised hand.

"And since there's more than one airplane in the airport wanting to land or take off, you need air traffic control, correct?" McNally asked. "Too many planes taking off, landing and crossing over the runways would be quite dangerous, wouldn't you think? And wouldn't a good pilot have some knowledge of his people—the ground crew, mechanics and everyone else who makes sure everything checks out before he flies?"

After another long pause, Plan appeared to realize that McNally was expecting an answer to this last question. "Well, yes." His voice was almost a whisper.

Leaning forward in his chair, McNally said somberly, "Let me relate this 'good flight' to your role here. As Mr. Plan, you are the pilot of the new Changes that are in your organization's airspace. Because you've never seen a bad idea, you are setting your organization up for what I call 'death by a thousand initiatives.' Prioritization must return to the organization and you must practice traffic control for Change. Your people and Budget can only handle a certain number of Changes at one time. And you must get in control of your processes. Infrastructure, Measurement and Prioritization must be on the same page when Change is getting ready to take off. And you, Plan, as the pilot, are ultimately responsible for the trip. While you should have an expectation that your crew and others will do their jobs well, Accountability must be on board also. Do you know Aidan Accountability?"

"I've heard of him but I've never met him," Plan said meekly.

"Not surprising," McNally responded. "I suppose you were up in the clouds yesterday when Change was murdered?"

"Yes."

"Well, consider yourself grounded until this investigation is completed." McNally stood up and stared hard at Plan. "You're dismissed," he said.

Back in his office, Plan took off his leather aviator jacket and tossed it onto a chair. Sitting down at his desk, he stared at a blank sheet of paper. Several times he put his pen to it but the words would not come. *Who does Agent McNally think he is, talking to me like that? Does he really think I don't care about Change's success? Of course I care,* he thought. His focus returned to his blank paper. He had decided to be more tactical and develop a detailed change implementation plan. Still, he was stumped. *Who could I get to help me with this?* he wondered.

It never occurred to Plan that he should talk to ACME's employees—the people most impacted by Change—to help develop the implementation plan. Apparently he'd never learned a fundamental lesson about Change leadership:

*

Those Who Plan The Battle
Rarely Battle The Plan.

*

Suspect #9: Budget

BAILEY Budget was next on McNally's list. He had envisioned what Budget would look like— short, round and balding, with a bitter disposition. He couldn't have been more wrong. At first he thought the woman who walked into the room was in the wrong place, but she introduced herself with a warm smile.

"I'm Bailey Budget. You must be Agent McNally. It's a pleasure to meet you."

McNally stood and shook her hand. "Pleasure to meet you, ma'am," he said. He wondered if he was blushing.

"Terrible, terrible thing," she said as she sat down. "Change was a real asset to our organization."

"Did you know him well?" McNally inquired, willing himself to the task at hand.

"Does anyone ever really know anyone well?" she asked, leaning back in her chair and staring at the ceiling.

"I suppose you report to Spence Sponsorship?"

"Yes, yes," she said absently. "If you want to get to who reports to whom, that's what it says on the organizational chart, but you and I know that when you hire someone who knows what she's doing it's better to just stay out of her way. Mr. Sponsorship stays out of my way."

"What was your working relationship with Change?" asked McNally.

"The same as my working relationship with everyone else here," Budget replied unemotionally, her eyes fixed on McNally. "I ultimately carry the weight of fiscal responsibility for ACME on my shoulders. That's what I was hired to do—to ensure that our investors get a return on their investment. I have to balance costs with revenue. People in the organization submit capital requests and I weigh them against the criteria we have established. I treated Change the same way I treated everyone else."

"Is it safe to assume, then, that you practice zero-based budgeting here?" McNally asked nonchalantly.

"Why, Agent McNally," she said with a sardonic smile, "you've been taking a mail-order accounting course, haven't you? Yes, we do. We do indeed. You see, most of our managers here do okay in their respective areas. I mean, they can manage their staffing, scheduling and the technical components of their jobs, but they don't see the big picture. Their focus is on the needs of their own departments. They don't have the ability to pull back and manage the priorities of the whole organization."

McNally was starting not to like this woman. With unbridled sarcasm he said, "So that's what you do? Manage the priorities of the whole organization?"

She simply said, "Yes, it's my responsibility."

McNally retorted, "Is it truly an issue of ability, or is it perhaps that you have not trained, or you do not trust, managers at ACME to evaluate trade-offs in terms of what the company is going to invest in?"

"Agent, Agent, Agent," she said as if talking to a child. "You really are naive, aren't you? I trust that the managers will do what they were hired to do. But do you really believe they can see the organization as I do?"

McNally redirected the conversation back to the subject at hand. "I've had the opportunity to look at the purchase orders submitted to you by Change over the past three months and you denied virtually every one of his requests." He waited for Budget to speak, but she did not respond. "Change understood fiscal responsibility. He had documentation on all of his purchase requests that were for any significant dollar amount. I've looked at his notes and he had calculated a return on investment on all of them. Can you explain why you didn't approve any of these requests?"

"Of course I can," she said emphatically.

"Let's hear it," McNally replied.

For the first time, Bailey Budget changed her tone of voice and spoke less dismissively. "You just don't seem to understand that I am actually helping the organization, do you? One of my key roles is to prevent the funding of a Change like the one that just died."

Agent McNally was ready to arrest Budget for murder and read her her rights, but he refrained. "Tell me more," he said, for the first time wanting to hear more from Budget.

She continued. "I am a firm believer that the amount of money I invest in a given Change should be in direct proportion to the investment of effort and quality of work being done by Mr. Sponsorship, Ms. Vision, Mr. Urgency, Mr. Change Leadership Team—we call him Pecs—Mr. Plan, Mr. Commitment, Ms. Culture, and Mr. Accountability. If these characters aren't doing what's necessary to enable Change, there is no reason for me to commit any funds to a Change that's destined to fail."

McNally didn't want to admit it, but he was starting to agree with Budget. He had no further questions for her.

Budget picked up her bag from the chair beside her, pulled out her compact case and freshened her lipstick. When she finished, she tucked the compact into her bag and stood up. Meeting McNally's eyes, she said in a very polite voice, "Agent McNally, it's been a pleasure meeting you. Give me a call when you've solved the case."

She walked out without looking back.

A Vision of Death

AGENT McNally had booked a cheap hotel close to the ACME organization earlier that day. After buying dinner at a fast-food drive-through, he checked into his room. The room was fairly clean and had the basics—bed, TV, desk and bathroom. He pulled out his sandwich and fries, laid them on the desk and flipped through the TV channels. As usual, nothing interesting was on. He decided to thumb through Change's file as he began eating. He found a scribbled note in Change's handwriting:

What I can do is to tap into the skills, ideas and energy of staff members throughout ACME so that they see me as valuable, not as disruptive.

McNally tossed the note down and realized that Change possessed a rare talent: respect for the people he was trying to influence.

• • • •

McNally was sitting in the conference room in the same chair in which Change had died. As he was waiting for his first interview of the morning, he reviewed his case notes.

Suddenly, he smelled an odd odor. He was having some trouble breathing now and his heart was racing. He ran to the door. It was locked. He pounded the door and screamed.

I'm the only one here, he thought. His eyes were now burning and he was feeling light-headed.

The next thing he knew, he was lying on his back on the floor. He gasped. He was drifting in and out of consciousness. When he opened his eyes, a circle of faces was leaning over him. He saw Culture, Commitment, Sponsorship, Pecs, Communication, Urgency, Vision, Plan, Budget and some guy he didn't recognize staring down blankly at him. The medical examiner broke up the circle, got down on one knee and put two fingers to McNally's neck. After a few seconds the doctor frowned and shook his head. "Too late," he said. "He's dead."

McNally tried to speak, to say, "No, it's a mistake—I'm alive!" But no words came out. He gave it all he had and tried to scream.

• • • •

McNally jerked upright in bed, awakened by his own scream. He was breathing like he'd run a four-minute mile. His sheets were wet with sweat. Now he realized where he was. It had been only a dream. He wiped the sweat from his forehead and his breathing began to slow. The clock read 5:17 A.M.

He got up, lit a cigar and sat on the edge of the bed. *Is this how Change felt when he died?* he wondered. He sat staring at the floor for several minutes. Finally he put out his cigar and headed for the shower. He had more work to do.

Suspect #10: Trainer

WHEN Terry Trainer entered the room for his interview, Agent McNally was appalled. The man's shirt was untucked and stained. His baseball cap was on backward; he was unshaven and vigorously chewing gum. Agent summed up Trainer's appearance with one word: *sloppy.*

Trainer sat down, looked at McNally and said without inflection, "What's happening?"

McNally sat up in his chair, an unconscious attempt to come across as a professional to this disheveled creature. "You are the trainer here, I understand," McNally opened.

"Yep, that's me," replied Trainer. He put one fist in the air and without any evidence of enthusiasm said, "Go, ACME team."

"And what was your relationship with Change?" inquired McNally.

"Front office guy, Change was," replied Trainer as he pushed his chair back and put both feet on the table. "Nice enough guy, I guess, but a little too far removed to understand the game, if you ask me."

"Game?" queried McNally.

"You know—the game."

McNally just stared at him.

"Sorry," Trainer continued, "I guess you've never played." The incessant gum chewing was driving McNally crazy. "Here's how it's played. Spence Sponsorship and Victoria Vision—those front office folks—bring in a new Change. I meet with this Change guy, figure out which ball field he wants to play on and then I assemble the team. Get them ready for the game."

"Okay, let's narrow that down. What's the most important thing you do at ACME?"

"Training," replied Trainer, again with a lack of emotion.

"Could you elaborate on that?"

"We make sure the team has the skills and commitment needed for the Change."

"'We'?" urged McNally.

"Isabella Incentive comes to a lot of the practices. She's more like a cheerleader. Doesn't really know the rules and mechanics of the game," replied Trainer.

"These practices," asked McNally, "what are they like? How often do you do them? How long do they last?"

"Depends," said Trainer philosophically. "Sometimes we'll just have one practice. We've got a lot of talented players here, but many of them had to take on new positions with Change. They needed practice before being thrown into the game. Mr. Change always wanted me to practice the team longer. I was committed to doing what I could to give the players the new skills they needed. Unfortunately, my commitment was stronger than Bailey Budget's commitment. She's just another one of those front office stuffed shirts. You'd think they would take the time to talk to one another. One says practice, practice, practice. The other says cut, cut, cut. But what do I know? I'm just Trainer."

"Where were you when Change was murdered?" McNally asked.

"In my office watching ESPN highlights," replied Trainer without any sign of embarrassment.

McNally asked, "Have you ever considered being trained yourself?"

"Not sure I catch your drift," Trainer replied.

"It seems to me that the only way the team wins is when you and everyone are on the same page. Clearly, that's not happening right now. What if you and Spence Sponsorship were aligned on what the players needed to develop new skills and commitment to Change? What if you worked with Sponsorship to build a compelling case that Bailey Budget couldn't deny? A good trainer could help you develop the skills you need to work more effectively with Sponsorship and Budget," McNally said.

"Really, a trainer could help me with that?" he asked.

Agent McNally didn't know whether to laugh or cry. "Yes, in fact a good trainer could help all of you—Culture, Commitment, Sponsorship, Change Leadership Team, Communication, Urgency, Vision, Plan and Budget—to get on the same page and work more effectively as a team."

McNally left Trainer to ponder the possibilities.

Suspect #11: Incentive

AGENT McNally looked at his watch and, realizing he had a few minutes before his next interview, decided to step outside for a cigar. It was no longer raining, but it was cold and the sky was gray. He buttoned up his coat, lit his cigar, took a long drag on it and began to think about his next suspect, Isabella Incentive.

McNally knew that Change's chances of survival in the organization were lessened if Incentive was not behind him. He was also aware that when many people thought of Incentive, they immediately thought of money. It was true that Incentive sometimes used money as an inducement for people to accept Change, but McNally's experience had taught him that Incentive had a lot of other options to promote the acceptance of Change and that money was not always the most important one.

Incentive was almost always liked by most of the people in the organization, at least at first. McNally remembered some cases in which Incentive was a top suspect in the murder of Change. It was when Incentive got out of alignment with Performance Management and Culture. When Incentive has a practice of rewarding work behaviors that are inconsistent with the foundation that is powered by Culture and the standards established by Performance Management, the stage is set for the perfect organizational storm.

McNally heard his name and turned to see Anna at the door.

"Your next appointment is here," she said.

He took a final drag on his cigar and headed back inside.

McNally entered the conference room with his coat hanging over his arm. An attractive woman met his gaze. She smiled and said, "Hello."

"Good afternoon," responded McNally. "I'm sure you know I want to ask you some questions about Change."

Her smile faded and her eyes welled up with tears. He found a box of tissues and handed the box to her, asking softly, "Were you two close?"

Incentive wiped her eyes and blew her nose. She made a weak attempt at a smile and said, "Yes, we were."

Some moments went by. McNally was about to ask another question but Incentive volunteered, "I considered him to be a close friend. We worked together virtually every week since he got here."

"What type of work?"

"Well," replied Incentive, "Change had come up with two really good ideas. Don't ask me to tell you more. I really don't understand the details behind what he was proposing. But Change did. He made a strong business case for his proposals to Change Leadership Team and both of his ideas were ultimately endorsed."

"Did Urgency help him with the business case?" McNally asked.

"I can't say I remember that Urgency was involved. Right after each endorsement Change came in to my office and asked for my help. His first idea involved one department where Change had spent more time and, I think, had a pretty good read on the management style there—something he called 'followership.' I'd never really heard that term before but Change explained that unless we could tap into the hearts and minds of the people who were going to be affected by what he was proposing, we probably would not be successful." Again Incentive began to dab at her welling eyes with a tissue.

She went on. "That's where he wanted my help—to try to find the motivators that would cause those employees to embrace Change. You see, my job here is to reinforce desired work behaviors that support Change."

"Did you help him?" asked McNally.

"Yes. Well, some. I think so. You know, it's really difficult to say because the new expectations haven't been in place long enough for us to know for sure. I'm sure I was able to help some with the embracing part, though."

"What motivators did you use?" inquired McNally.

Incentive brightened. "First," she said cheerfully, "we looked at monetary rewards. Change had calculated the dollar amount of savings ACME would realize if his proposals were implemented and he'd even calculated the effect on cash flow. Once he told me that, I suggested that a nominal amount of money might be motivating for some employees. I should let you know that we pulled Peter Performance Management into this discussion right away. We felt that this type of motivator without a relationship to Performance Management might backfire on us." She stopped and McNally noticed a change in her demeanor.

"What was the outcome?" McNally inquired.

"We spent several weeks off and on in meetings creating a program that linked Change, Performance Management and the new behaviors we expected. We made sure it was fair and measurable, but the whole thing got nixed."

"By whom?"

"Bailey Budget," replied Incentive. She did not mask her anger.

McNally reflected that Budget had certainly taken the efficiency value to heart, and Incentive obviously resented that.

"What else did you advise Change to do?" he asked Incentive.

"I was able to sit in on the presentation that Change gave to the leadership team, where he made the business case for what he was proposing. I thought if Change could convince those folks to do anything other than what we've always done, then he should do a presentation to the employees in the departments that were going to be most impacted. Not necessarily the exact same presentation, but one that showed them there was some thoughtful analysis that led to the recommendation to integrate Change."

"Did he do it?"

"He did," answered Incentive. "But you know what? Before he did, I know he enlisted the support of Pecs, Spence Sponsorship and a number of others. If there is one thing Change did well, it was to try to pull the team together who would support him in these initiatives."

"Do you know anybody who would want to kill Change?" McNally asked.

After a few seconds she responded, "It's not my style to be negative."

McNally retorted, "This is a murder case. If you have any information, positive or negative, it is your obligation to communicate it to me."

Her eyes welled up again and she stated, "It is pure speculation on my part."

"Understood."

"You already know, I suppose, my feelings about Ms. Budget. And while I'm aware that money is not the only motivator, I think it would have helped. I had the feeling Ms. Budget wanted Change out of here."

"Who else?" asked McNally.

"Peter Performance Management—and I think Carolina Culture could have been involved too. She's supposedly here all the time but no one sees her. Want to know why? Because she's meeting all day behind closed doors in Bailey Budget's office. Those two are in cahoots, I tell you."

"Anybody else?"

"Well, maybe. Some might think I'm crazy, but I think if it wasn't Bailey Budget or Carolina Culture, it could be gang related."

"Gang related?" McNally asked with surprise.

"Yeah. The other initiative didn't get off the ground so well."

"What happened?"

"I heard the manager of that department got wind of the proposed initiative and pulled some of his key employees aside to instruct them on how to sabotage it. That's just what I've heard through the rumor mill, but I've known that manager for years and he has a history of similar behavior. He's sly, though—never gets caught. He has built up some loyalty in his department so no one confronts the behavior."

McNally looked at his watch and realized it was time for his next interview. "I may need to talk with you again," he said, getting up from the table.

"Is that all for now, then?" Incentive sounded surprised.

"For now—but I'll be in touch with you."

Wiping her eyes and blowing her nose, Isabella Incentive got up and left.

Reflections on Plan, Budget, Trainer and Incentive

MCNALLY was beginning to wonder if any Change had ever stood a chance of being successfully initiated and integrated—not to mention sustained—in this organization. McNally was already well into his second notebook, all the while hoping that another organization, if not this one, could benefit from his learnings. He reviewed what he'd written about the past four suspects, starting with Plan.

PLAN

Plan was no friend to Change:

- He never worked out the details. He focused on the big picture. But it was the details that raised people's implementation concerns. As they got into integrating Change, people were astounded that no one had ever thought about Change from their perspective.

- He never planned for early wins. As a result, it was difficult to show performance gains in the beginning. With little to celebrate at the outset, those who liked to sit on the fence used the early marginal results as an easy excuse to resist Change.
- He never included those being asked to change in the planning process as a way to improve the plan and gain their buy-in.

BUDGET

Budget was really suspicious. A lot of her colleagues thought she murdered Change:

- She spent almost no money on creating the infrastructure that would support Change.
- She had too much power over the other players on the leadership team who needed to help Change succeed.

- She did approve—under some heavy pressure from Sponsorship—a few requests. They didn't make much sense but they kept the heat off her for a while. For example, Plan asked Budget for some consultants. They got together for a few days in a war room and created a big document, but they didn't consult anyone who had a realistic sense of what was needed to fully integrate Change into the organization. And of course, Budget allocated a few dollars to Trainer for training, because she knew she would be ridiculed if Change was tried without any training to support the effort.

TRAINER

Trainer contributed to the demise of Change as well:

- He made a halfhearted attempt at training those being asked to change, but the training didn't stand a chance for a number of reasons:

  - The business processes and technology had never been piloted, so the kinks were never worked out prior to training.

- Due to his sloppy appearance and less than optimal skill set, Trainer had little credibility with the people he was responsible for developing.

INCENTIVE

Incentive was at the very least an accessory to the crime:

- She tried to help Change, but really didn't make her relationships with Culture and Performance Management work, so Budget shot down most of her ideas for supporting Change.

Suspect #12:
Performance Management

PETER Performance Management was next on the list. McNally had received a note from Anna earlier in the morning that Performance Management could meet him at 11:00 A.M. but they would need to meet in Performance Management's office in the HR department.

McNally was glad for the break from the conference room. He exited through the conference room door and took an elevator to the basement level. After a long stroll down a dimly lit hallway, he found a warren of small offices tucked into the corner of the building. McNally wandered in, searching for someone who might be able to point him to Performance Management's office.

McNally poked his head into the first occupied office and found a stocky, middle-aged man sorting through a towering stack of paperwork. The man looked up with wary eyes.

"And you are?" he asked.

"Agent Mike McNally, here for an eleven o'clock with Mr. Performance Management."

"That's me. Have a seat." He nodded toward the no-frills chair in the corner.

McNally took a seat and scanned the office. Apart from the dinged-up metal filing cabinets and stacks of paper covering Performance Management's desk, it was fairly neat. Still, something wasn't quite right, but he couldn't put his finger on it.

Performance Management cleared his desk, placing his paperwork on the credenza behind him, which was already piled high with several more stacks of paper. He looked at McNally and managed a tight smile.

"Hey, thanks for meeting me back here," he said. "I'm under the gun to get some projects done. It's always a hassle at this time of year because performance evaluations are due. Everyone always waits until the last minute to turn them in, so I'm always swamped." He reached eagerly for a bowl of wrapped candies at the corner of his desk. "Care for any?" he asked, pushing the bowl toward McNally. "They're tropical—guava, mango, passion fruit. Sugar free, so no guilt."

"Thanks but no thanks," said McNally.

"I'd prefer a cigarette myself," said Performance Management with a smile.

"Nervous?" McNally asked.

"More like stressed," he replied. "As you can see, I'm buried in work."

It was a good opening for McNally. "How long have you worked here?" he asked.

"Twenty years this July," Performance Management responded.

"You like what you do?"

"Sure, sure. It's hard work but rewarding."

"I may be asking the obvious here, but what do you do here?" McNally asked.

Performance Management sat back in his chair and unwrapped his candy. The sound of crinkling cellophane filled the small space. He finally offered, "My responsibility is to track the outcomes we expect from people. Every year we insist that leaders throughout the organization lay out the goals for everyone on their teams. Then twice a year they're supposed to chart people's progress on those goals. Have a meeting. Provide feedback."

"So where do you come in?" McNally asked.

"As you can see," he said, sweeping his hand toward the towering stacks of paper, "I collect all the documentation. Most of the leaders here—I'm sure you've met a few of them—tend to procrastinate. You've probably talked to Sponsorship or Urgency. They're two of the most notorious when it comes to getting their performance evals in on time." He shook his head disdainfully and popped the candy into his mouth.

"How was your relationship with Change?" McNally asked.

"Oh, fine, fine. Change and I were okay. We were on the same page most of the time, if you know what I mean. In general, I liked many of the Changes that came through, but I must admit I've lost my fair share of sleep over them."

"Because?" McNally prompted.

"I guess because almost everything associated with Change is new and I'm usually anxious about whether we'll succeed in communicating to people all the new things they're supposed to be working on. We never take something off people's plates when we ask them to make a Change. Then when we do the performance evaluation, people haven't accomplished their goals because months ago Change started to take up all their time.

"It's a mess," he continued with a sigh. "I have a lot of doubts about whether or not people can learn everything they need to learn to make Change a success."

"So you worry about the organization but not so much about yourself?" McNally asked.

Performance Management lowered his eyes and sucked on his candy. "To be honest, I often worry about whether I can possibly measure up to the new standards established by the Change."

"Any thoughts on who might have killed Change?"

"Yep," replied Performance Management, looking up and nodding. There was a long silence. Finally he said quietly, "I think Bailey Budget did it."

"Budget, eh?" replied McNally.

"Yep, pretty sure it was Budget."

He had McNally's interest but the agent nonchalantly rested his head on his hand and said, "So, what's her motive? Why would Budget want Change dead?"

Performance Management didn't answer but got up from his chair, walked over to one of the filing cabinets, pulled out a stack of papers and dropped them in front of McNally on the desk.

"So, what are these?" questioned McNally.

"Purchase requests from the past six months."

McNally perused the purchase requests. He did not tell Performance Management that he had already seen copies of these in Change's file. They all were submitted by Change and each one of them was rubber-stamped DENIED with Budget's signature below the stamp. McNally looked up at Performance Management.

"People want Change but they're not willing to pay for it. And Bailey Budget, well, she's just"— he paused to search for the right word—"tight, if you get my drift. What Change was trying to do required training and retooling in some areas. Look at the purchase orders. He wasn't asking for the moon, just the basics." Performance Management bit down hard on his candy, crunching it loudly between his teeth.

"Most of these purchase orders related to the four main Change initiatives?" asked McNally.

"Four? Who said there were four?"

"Spence Sponsorship did."

Performance Management rolled his eyes and stated, "That guy spends so much time looking in the mirror, he can't see past himself. Two. We have, or had, two major initiatives going on."

McNally asked, "You think Budget acted alone?"

An amused smile came over Performance Management's face. "If you find a smoking gun, I think it will have Budget's fingerprints all over it, but—" He stopped midsentence.

"But?" offered McNally.

"She may have had an accomplice, though I doubt you'll ever find any evidence."

"Can you be more specific?" inquired McNally.

"Have you met Culture yet?"

"Yes."

"I've been here almost twenty years and I can't say that I've seen her more than eight or ten times, but word on the street is that she is extremely influential. Keeping a watchful eye on spending has been a part of her way of doing things for as long as I can remember."

"So are you saying that Budget just did her bidding?" asked McNally.

"Something like that," Performance Management replied. "As far as I'm concerned, she's probably just as guilty as Budget is. I'm generally not one to complain. I come in and take care of my business. But with these Changes, when other people don't do their jobs, I'm the one that looks bad."

"Look," said McNally, "we need to keep this conversation between us. I still have a lot of investigating to do and I don't want this to get out in the rumor mill."

"No problem," replied Performance Management. "In fact, I was going to ask you to extend me the same courtesy. I really can't afford to lose my job."

McNally suddenly realized what wasn't quite right about the office: its location and condition. The HR department was tucked away in a remote underground corner of ACME's headquarters. The furniture was shabby—not shabby chic—and there wasn't a computer in sight. Just a lot of gray metal filing cabinets. Most of them looked like they hadn't been touched in decades.

"You use all these cabinets?" McNally asked.

"Yeah, those cabinets are where we file the performance evaluation forms. There's a ton of them, believe me."

"Even in this day and age of electronic filing?"

"There was talk of a Change initiative involving electronic records management, but I think that one died too," said Performance Management with a cynical laugh.

That laughter lingered in McNally's mind as he said good-bye and made his way to the elevator through the dim hallway.

Suspect #13: Accountability

ACCOUNTABILITY was sitting at the table when Agent McNally returned to the conference room. He looked younger than McNally had thought he would. He had to be in his mid- to late twenties. A preppy type.

"Hello, I'm Agent Mike McNally," he offered.

"Aidan Accountability," the young man replied, rising to shake hands.

"Please sit down," McNally said, motioning toward the chair as he took a seat across the table. "So I suppose you know what I want to talk to you about?"

"Sure. That's no secret."

"Who do you report to?" inquired McNally.

"Spence Sponsorship is my counselor."

"And how often do you two meet?"

"Oh, we met right after I was hired. He was very clear on what he wanted me to do. Haven't seen him since." Accountability's tone was as dismissive as his answer.

"How long have you been with the organization?"

"Just over six months. In fact, I started the same day as Change. Went through orientation together," he said enthusiastically.

McNally asked, "So did you work with him much?"

"Oh yeah, we worked with him all the time."

"'We'?" McNally inquired.

"My department," said Accountability.

"You have a department?"

"Of course," he said. "The position I have was open for almost two years. It's a difficult job and I understand they had trouble finding someone qualified for the money they were offering, so as soon as I got my feet wet, I hired Delegation, Follow-up and Consequences. There was, and still is, a lot to be done in my department."

McNally inquired, "So how did you get Budget to go for that?"

"I will say that it took some convincing. She's quite, um, frugal, if you know what I mean. Delegation is really the only one we're paying, and he gets minimum wage. Follow-up is just interning here, and Consequences is here on some kind of grant."

Just then there was a knock on the door. Anna stuck her head in and said to Accountability, "Please excuse the interruption, but the manager of IT just called looking for you. He said it was urgent." She closed the door and was gone.

"Pardon me for a moment," Accountability said. He picked up the phone and punched four numbers. McNally heard only Accountability's side of the conversation.

"Hello, Delegation? Yeah, it's me. Listen, the IT manager supposedly has an issue that needs to be taken care of right away. *(Pause)* No, I'm in a meeting with Agent McNally and I can't leave. *(Pause)* I understand you have a lot of things on your plate but. . . . *(Pause)* Listen, take Follow-up with you. Make sure you have a good assessment of what they need, then let him deal with it. *(Pause)* Again? How many times has he called in sick this month? *(Long pause)* Okay, okay. Just take Consequences then. *(Pause)* I am well aware he's not good with people. Pull him aside before you go and tell him you just want his presence. You don't want him talking. Tell him you want him to roll up his sleeves, cross his arms and flex his biceps. *(Pause)* Yeah, he'll like that." Accountability chuckled. *(Pause)* "No, it's not necessary to call me back. Just take care of it."

Accountability hung up the phone, looked at McNally and commented, "If you want something done right, you just have to do it yourself."

McNally was having difficulty reconciling this comment with the unilateral conversation he had just heard. He looked at Accountability and said, "Excuse me just a moment."

McNally left the room and returned about five minutes later. He took his chair and said, "Do you have any idea who killed Change?"

"Yeah, Change," Accountability replied.

Confused, McNally responded, "Yes, do you know who killed Change?"

"Oh, I'm sorry. I wasn't very clear. I think Change killed Change," he replied. After a short pause he added, "Suicide."

"You think he committed suicide?" McNally inquired with interest.

"Sure. It's the only reasonable explanation. There were some folks here, I admit, that didn't really care for Change, but I can't think of anyone who would go so far as to kill him. Besides, in retrospect, he displayed all the signs. Wish I had picked up on them then. Maybe there was something I could have done."

"Signs?" nudged McNally.

"When Change started he was, you know, all gung ho. I mean, that guy had energy. But the last six weeks or so he was like a different person. He was here all hours of the day. I don't know when he slept. He was irritable all the time and he had lost weight. We used to have lunch together but he didn't seem to have time anymore. I heard that one of his initiatives was going okay, but I don't think the other initiative was moving along well at all. Word on the street is that the guys in that department had it in for Change. They are a pretty tough group." Accountability paused for a moment and then offered, "Depression. That is what it was. Depression. Change was under an extreme amount of pressure and I think he got overwhelmed and sunk into a deep depression." As Accountability finished, he stared off into the distance.

McNally had immediately dismissed what he considered to be an idiotic theory. This was not a suicide. It was definitely murder. But something Accountability said did intrigue him.

"You said you heard that one initiative wasn't going well. That was the word on the street?" McNally asked.

Accountability looked baffled. "Well, yeah," he said, "but what's that got to do with anything?"

McNally no longer tried to hide his brewing agitation. He got up and began pacing the length of the room as he spoke. "I don't understand how you could know so little about these two initiatives. Change needed your expertise and you apparently had no idea what was even happening. You—"

"Look, that's not fair!" Accountability interrupted. "I—"

McNally put his hand up and resumed. "Let me fill in the blanks for you. Change asked for your help. You were certainly willing but you were having trouble finding time on your calendar. After all, there is still—how did you say it?—a lot to be done in your department. But you had the answer. Delegation could do it and if he needed help he could always enlist Follow-up and Consequences."

Accountability sat stunned and silent. McNally put both hands on the table and leaned in. "You have made a mockery of the very job you were hired for. Your job requires maturity and you just don't have it. When I left the room, I spent a few minutes reviewing the minutes of some of your meetings and found exactly what I expected." McNally's voice was getting louder and again he began to pace. "Issues came up. You assigned a person to action. Even declared a time frame for completion. But when I tracked these issues through the next set of meeting minutes, the issues just dropped off the face of the earth. Nothing. Did they get resolved?" he asked rhetorically. "Doubtful," he answered.

McNally could have said much more but he bit his tongue. What he had to say would not move the investigation forward. He took one more look at Accountability. The suspect's face was now red and he stared at the floor. McNally paused to allow Accountability an opportunity to respond. He did not.

McNally slammed the door as he left the room.

Super Cops and Stakeholders

AGENT McNally was on his way to meet with the employees in a conference room near the rear of the building. He knew there were stakeholders in every organization and was disappointed in himself for not remembering that the employees— the ones Change impacts the most—were the primary stakeholders. As he turned the corner of a hallway, he encountered a scene that stopped him cold. Agent McNally had spent his career working with police forces, so he was quite familiar with their routines and practices. But not once had he ever seen this inside a building. What he was staring at could be described only as a roadblock. The hallway had turned eerily dark, but there was enough light for him to make out the images: A sawhorse fully blocking the passageway. A large motorcycle parked parallel to the wall. And the most menacing police officer he had ever seen.

The officer was dressed in full police regalia including a helmet and dark sunglasses. His massive arms were folded in a manner that communicated "Don't even think about messing with me." As Agent McNally took a step forward, the police officer raised his arm in a gesture to stop.

"I'm just trying to get to a meeting—" McNally began.

The police officer slid his hand closer to the gun at his side and took a step forward.

"No problem," McNally said. He backed away and began looking for another route.

By the time McNally circled around to the conference room, four employees were waiting for the three o'clock meeting. Agent McNally apologized for his tardiness and began the introductions. David and Karen were from a department that had been doing pretty well integrating Change. Mark and Stephanie were from another department that had been resisting Change. McNally had picked these four from the entries in Change's calendar.

McNally opened the meeting. "I'm going to be very direct with you and I expect you to be direct with me," he said. "I'm investigating Change's murder. So far I have made at least one mistake in the investigation."

The four looked at him wide-eyed.

"My mistake was that I didn't talk with you first. I've spent a day and a half interviewing the leaders and managers, each of whom—"

McNally paused. He was about to say "each of whom has danced around most of my questions and some of whom are not competent enough to get a job anywhere else," but he restrained himself.

"Eh . . . let me just apologize for my oversight," he said instead. "According to Change's calendar, you four spent the most time with him during the last few weeks of his life. I am hoping you have information that may help me with my investigation." One by one, he looked each of them in the eye.

The four exchanged glances. Finally Karen said, "Change was okay. I didn't like him at first. The stuff he was talking about doing was scary, but, you know, the more time he spent with us explaining things and finding out from us how things were working, the more sense he made. If it weren't for all the barriers, I think we could have worked better with Change."

"What barriers do you mean?" inquired McNally.

Stephanie replied, "You must have seen them. Well, maybe not," she said hesitantly. After a long pause, she said, "Most employees can see them. A few supervisors can see them but managers and above rarely see them. But trust me, they are real." She turned to the others for support.

David broke the silence. "Super Cop," he said with a nod.

McNally replied, "I think I just saw him. Pretty intimidating."

"Just one?" said Mark with a snicker. "They're all over the place. Just when it seems like we're going down the right path—making progress with a new idea—a Super Cop shows up, blocking everything. They've been here forever. They might as well post 'We've Never Done It That Way Before' signs in the halls. It's unbelievable to me that a lot of the employees see them, but most of the managers and leaders don't seem to know they exist."

Karen asked, "Have you seen the guy walking around with the whip in his hand? He sort of looks like a Roman soldier," she added.

"No," replied McNally.

"Well, that's Reprimand. He shows up only when an employee makes a mistake. Starts cracking his whip and informing everyone how stupid they are. He disappears when Incentive comes around, but she's not around that much."

"How about Hypocrite?" Mark asked. "Have you seen him?"

"I'm not sure. What does he look like?" responded McNally.

"That's just the thing. He's sort of a chameleon. Never looks the same."

"But," interjected David, "he's easy enough to recognize. He always says one thing and then does another. He gives us all these 'we, we, we' speeches and then he's off on his own doing just the opposite of what he preaches."

There was a moment of silence as McNally pictured this.

Stephanie broke in. "The one that gets me the most, though, is Convertible."

"Why do you call him Convertible?" asked McNally.

"Because he's always driving everything top down," she replied.

McNally laughed but stopped quickly when he realized no one else was laughing. "Sorry," he said apologetically.

"Oh, that's okay," answered Stephanie. "It's just that everything is his way or the highway. Some of his ideas are actually not bad, but then he wants to direct all the details even though he is clueless about the day-to-day operations. If he would only allow us to be involved."

McNally thought she was going to say more but she just sat there looking wistful. "I must admit," McNally said, "all of these characters you have to deal with—Super Cop, Reprimand, Hypocrite and Convertible—do make things quite confusing."

"Now you know how we feel," Stephanie responded.

McNally talked with the employees for at least another hour. Then he picked up the phone and asked Anna to arrange one more meeting.

The Autopsy Report

LATER that day, Agent McNally stood outside the building alternating between drags on his cigar and sips of his coffee. It was starting to get dark and a light drizzle was coming down. McNally pulled his coat up tight and leaned against the building. He was wishing he had talked to the employees earlier.

The door opened and the sound of Anna's voice pulled him from his thoughts.

"Agent McNally, it's the medical examiner on the phone. He wants to talk to you."

He took a final drag on the cigar and flipped it to the ground. As he walked inside, Anna said, "I'll put the call through to the conference room."

The phone was ringing when he walked into the room. He hit the speaker button and put his coffee down. "McNally here," he said. "That you, Doc?"

"Yep," Doc replied. "I've finished the autopsy. Thought I'd catch you up on where we are. Is this a good time?"

"Great," replied McNally. "Go ahead."

Doc began, "I'm going with between seven and nine A.M. as the time of death. Right now I'm listing cause of death as heart failure."

"Heart failure?" McNally interjected. "He died of natural causes?"

"Not so fast, Dick Tracy," said Doc with a chuckle. "The heart failure was the result of a type of poisoning."

"So you tested the fluid from the glass that spilled," McNally surmised. "What was it, arsenic?"

"Certainly, we tested the fluid," replied Doc. "But it was clean—just water."

This was starting to sound familiar to McNally. He said, "So, was it—"

"Yeah," Doc interrupted, "it was C-15."

Agent McNally reflected on some of his other cases. C-15 was the mysterious poison that was identified as the cause of death. At the time it was named, there were fifteen known related cases and the C stood for Change.

McNally asked, "Do they know any more about C-15 yet?"

"No, not really." Doc sounded disappointed. "The scientists are working on it but all they really know is that it acts slowly. Usually over one to two months. Based on anecdotal evidence, the only known associated symptoms are insomnia, anxiety, nervousness and weight loss. So I obtained Change's medical records. He had a required physical when he started at ACME. Healthy as a horse. All lab tests were normal and he had no significant problems in his medical history. I weighed him and he'd lost twenty-five pounds since then. And, oh yeah, his fingernails were chewed down to the quick."

McNally asked, "So the toxin finally built up enough that he had a heart attack?"

Doc replied, "Not a heart attack, a heart failure. A heart attack is generally caused by a long build-up of plaque or a clot in the coronary arteries, which blocks blood flow. No blood means no oxygen and the heart cells die. Change's coronary arteries were fine. When I say 'heart failure,' I literally mean that his heart just stopped beating."

"Wow," said McNally. "That's scary. Anything else?"

"Nope, not right now," Doc replied. "I've sent some tissue off for pathology but I'm pretty sure this is a C-15 case."

McNally thanked the doctor and asked him to let him know if anything else came up. He hung up the phone.

Meanwhile, in a pile on Doc's untidy desk, the current edition of *Perspectives in Forensics* was lying unread. An obscure article on page fifteen was titled "Trace Elements of C-15." The opening read:

C-15 has been identified as the toxin leading to heart failure and death in a number of Changes. Although much is still unknown about this toxin, scientists believe a number of trace elements make up this deadly substance and have recently identified three of those trace elements:

- *People leading the Change think that announcing him is the same as integrating him.*
- *People's concerns with Change are not surfaced or addressed.*
- *Those being asked to implement Change are not involved in the planning.*

Murderer Announced:
Invitation Only

ANNA had made all the arrangements. McNally had asked her to reserve a room and gather all the suspects for a 7:00 P.M. meeting. The room was in the front corner of the building. It was primarily used as a lounge for the leaders and managers, and could have comfortably accommodated thirty-five people. Anna had arranged some circular tables with four chairs at each table, and a number of chairs peppered the periphery of the room. In addition, there were two couches and a recliner.

McNally walked in a few minutes before seven o'clock and began arranging his notes at the podium as people started to arrive. At one point he looked up and found that no one would make eye contact with him.

Vision was standing at the window with her hands clasped behind her back, appearing oblivious to the crowd behind her.

Budget and Culture were side by side on one of the couches. They took turns whispering to each other.

Performance Management and Incentive had settled at one of the tables. Performance Management was sucking on a piece of candy. Incentive stared blankly.

Communication was sitting in one of the stray chairs, fiddling with her hearing aid. McNally had noticed a sign outside the door that read MURDERER ANNOUNCED HERE AT 7:00 P.M.: INVITATION ONLY, and assumed it was her work.

Pecs was sitting on one of the tables. He had enormous weights on his ankles. With what seemed to be considerable strain, he was practicing leg extensions.

Accountability, Delegation, Follow-up and Consequences sat at another table. McNally could not hear what they were saying but their body language led McNally to believe they were not happy with one another. He noticed that they kept pointing at each other.

Commitment could not seem to get comfortable. He constantly moved from seat to seat.

Trainer was still chomping his gum. He rested comfortably in an easy chair and methodically tossed a baseball up in the air.

Plan was making paper airplanes and floating them around the room.

Sponsorship appeared to be bored. McNally thought it may have been because he was not leading the meeting.

McNally noticed someone in the back but was having trouble recognizing him. He put on his glasses and was astounded to see the same unknown man who had stood over him in his dream. McNally motioned for Anna—who was seated at a table near the front—to come to the podium.

"Who is that small guy in the back of the room?" he asked in a whisper.

She looked to the back of the room and raised her eyebrows. "That's Fear," she said.

"Fear?" he asked.

"Yeah," she replied, "he just shows up sometimes. Doesn't really work here. I mean, he's not on the payroll or anything. He just shows up and no one seems to question his presence. Never says a word to anyone, but when he's around, people just seem to act different."

McNally considered whether it would be prudent to ask Fear to leave. Yet something told him that Fear's presence in this situation might be helpful.

Anna caught McNally's eye and tapped her watch. McNally cleared his throat and said, "It's seven o'clock, so let's begin. First, I want to thank all of you for rearranging your schedules to be here."

The door suddenly opened and Urgency scurried in. He mumbled his apologies as he found his seat.

McNally continued, "As you know, Change was killed recently and I've been talking to you and others over the past two days." He looked directly at Accountability and stated, "Just so there are no misconceptions, it was murder." Accountability seemed to be counting the laces on his shoes. "He was poisoned and the murderer is in this room."

The responses varied from silent questioning looks to loud gasps. Vision actually turned from the window and stared at McNally.

McNally continued, "I'm not as stupid as some of you think I am. I don't have an advanced degree, but what I do know is Change and people. I've spent my career studying both. Change is rarely accepted easily by any organization, but each of you had a responsibility to help him get integrated here.

"Ms. Vision," McNally said, raising his voice.

Vision jolted at the unexpected notice.

"Your job is to help others see the benefits of Change. To help them look beyond the present and into the future. You failed miserably."

Vision pulled the tissue again from her coat pocket and began cleaning her glasses. She did not look up.

"Mr. Urgency," McNally bellowed. "Change needed your support to make his integration a priority—to help him develop a compelling case for himself. Did you give him that support?" McNally asked rhetorically. "No, you were always late. You will probably be late for your own funeral.

"Mr. Sponsorship," McNally said, meeting his eyes. "The staff needed to know there was high-level executive backing for Change. That doesn't happen on a golf course or through a onetime announcement. It takes a good leadership team to support Change—one that you failed to build."

McNally walked to the window and spent a few moments looking at the sky before he turned back to his audience.

"Oh, there you are," McNally said, looking at Plan. "I expected you to have your head up in the clouds. That is where you spend most of your time, isn't it?

"And Ms. Culture," McNally said, lowering his voice. "Of all people, you could have been the one to set the tone and lay the groundwork for Change's success. But who you say you are and who you really are—well, they're really quite different, aren't they? You pop in and out of here like a ghost and expect people to respect you. Stop kidding yourself.

"And then there's your buddy, Ms. Budget," he continued. "Ms. fiscal responsibility."

McNally noticed that Fear was now propped on the arm of the couch, peering down at Budget.

McNally continued, "Budget, you know that Change rarely succeeds without proper funding. I'm surprised you don't have carpal tunnel syndrome from use of your 'denial' stamp. While you're correct that these other characters need to do their part before you approve funding, you never bothered letting them know why you were denying Change's many requests for it. If they knew your rationale, perhaps it would have motivated them to act differently.

"And then we have the illustrious Mr. Trainer." McNally made a dramatic sweep of the room with his hand. "This is all just a game to you. You have the unique opportunity to help the employees build their skills to support Change but instead you spend your time in your office watching ESPN. Here's the score, Trainer. You're a loser."

For the first time during the meeting, Trainer dropped his ball.

McNally moved his gaze to Accountability's table. "And here we have the pass-the-buck clan. You're a disgrace. Change needed your support to sustain the gains that had been made. People need Accountability when Change comes. You overused Delegation. And Follow-up just wasn't here enough. You used Consequences like a hammer and that's a tool that usually works only when Fear is present."

Fear was now standing behind Consequences, massaging his shoulders.

"But we know," McNally said as he turned to Incentive, "that there are a number of ways to motivate people to accept Change." His voice was not as harsh. "I'm not sure about motive, but you did have opportunity. You had the opportunity to push harder for Change in ways that the employees might accept him more readily. Just because there's dysfunction all around you," he said as he scanned the audience, "doesn't give you permission to give up."

McNally looked over at Communication. He wondered how much of the conversation she had heard while she was adjusting her hearing aid. He had the urge to begin with her by saying, "You have the right to remain silent," but thought better of it.

"Ms. Communication," he said, raising his volume, "Change needed a voice in the organization and you failed to consistently provide that. And just as he needed that voice to be successful, employees needed an ear. Someone to listen to their fears."

Fear was now in the back of the room, nodding his head in agreement.

"Someone to hear their concerns and their ideas," McNally continued. "In this, Ms. Communication, you failed." There was no doubt that she had heard him. Her eyes welled with tears.

McNally turned and met Pecs's eyes. Pecs stopped his leg extensions. McNally said, "Pecs, your ego is your Achilles' heel. Change needs a Change Leadership Team that will carry him throughout the organization. You took pride in holding him up, particularly in pumping him up in the beginning, but then it became all about you, didn't it? You wanted the acclaim, but you didn't want to do all the work."

Performance Management was next. McNally looked at him and said, "You do fairly good work in the context of the dysfunction here, but after this meeting I want you in Budget's office with those purchase orders for her reconsideration."

Commitment was the only one who had not been addressed. He was shifting uncomfortably in his chair. Fear hovered beside him like a shadow.

"Given the ineptitude of your colleagues, Mr. Commitment, you really didn't have a chance." Commitment was expecting more, but there McNally stopped. Fear moved away from his side.

McNally had set his watch on the podium for this moment. He looked down at it and waited out thirty seconds of silence. He wanted it to be an uncomfortable silence. Everyone in the room looked from one to another. Urgency paced faster. Fear began running around the room.

Suddenly Urgency stopped and called out, "I can't stand it anymore! You said someone in this room killed Change. Who was it?"

McNally took a deep breath and looked around the room. "In my opinion, all of you did," he said emphatically. "All of you killed Change. Most of you saw the crime scene. The spilled glass next to Change did not contain the poison. It was tested and it was clean. The poison that killed Change did so very slowly. I can't prove it but I believe the poison was neglect—your neglect. He tried to survive without the support he needed from you but ultimately, his is not a one-man job. He finally lost heart.

"I would arrest every one of you if I had enough evidence but . . ." His voice trailed off.

McNally organized his papers at the podium, put them in his briefcase and walked to the door. He looked back and said, "I'm confident you will eventually have another Change here. Look at my face. This is not a face you ever want to see again."

He turned his back to the crowd and left the room.

Change Lives!

THE next morning found Agent McNally at the cemetery. He had not slept well the night before. He felt he needed to pay his last respects. Change had no known next of kin. There had been no funeral, no eulogy and no community grieving. McNally could not let Change go like that.

He pulled his coat up to his neck as he approached a grave that had been paid for by the state. The morning was clear but a cold wind was blowing. He looked down at the simple grave.

After a few minutes of paying his respects, he got up and walked toward his car. His cell phone rang. "McNally here," he said into the phone.

It was Anna. "We've got another one," she said urgently.

McNally's heart sank. "Where's the body?" he said.

"Well, that's just it. There's not a body," she said with some excitement in her voice.

"What do you mean?" McNally demanded.

Anna replied, "It's another Change. This time it was a knife to the back and he's not dead. He's in ICU over at Memorial Hospital."

McNally replied quickly, "Tell them I'm on the way." He hung up, put his light on the hood of his car and gunned the motor. The wheels threw gravel as the car lurched away.

McNally glanced back through his rearview mirror. He saw Change's grave and then what must have been hundreds of graves just like it as far as the eye could see.

"Change," he said as he sped forward, "this one's for you."

Helping Change Thrive in Your Organization

UNDOUBTEDLY, you read this book wanting to know how you can successfully lead people through change. Up until now, you've learned a great deal about a cast of characters who can kill change. However, this same cast of characters has great power to help change thrive in an organization.

This chapter explores some of the best practices, linked to each character, that enable and sustain change in organizations like yours. Use these best practices and questions to identify where a given change is set up to succeed as well as where change may be at risk. Then develop an action plan to leverage your potential and address your risks.

1. **CULTURE.** Culture is defined as the predominant attitudes, beliefs and behavior patterns that characterize the organization. The role of culture is critical throughout the change process. Culture has the power to either enable and sustain the change or bury the change. To align culture to a change, you should:

- Determine how you can leverage the current culture to support, enable and sustain the change.
- Use sponsorship, accountability and incentive to reinforce the culture required to enable and sustain the change.
- Determine where the current culture is not aligned with the proposed change, and what actions are required to align the culture with the change.

ASK THESE QUESTIONS:

- How would you describe your organization's culture?
- In what ways is your organizational culture conducive to successful change?
- In what ways could your culture inhibit successful change? How difficult will it be to change the culture? What can you do to align the culture with the change?

2. **COMMITMENT.** Commitment describes a person's motivation and confidence to engage in the new behaviors required by the change initiative. To increase people's commitment to a change, you should:

- Provide forums for people to express their questions and concerns and then respond to those questions and concerns.
- Expand opportunities to increase the involvement and influence of those being asked to change. This produces long-term, sustainable commitment to a new way of doing business, rather than short-term compliance.
- Purposefully orchestrate opportunities for advocates of the change to contact those who have yet to make up their mind about the change.

ASK THESE QUESTIONS:

- Have the people being asked to change had an opportunity to express their questions and concerns? If not, how can you surface and address these questions and concerns?
- Have the people being asked to change had an opportunity to get involved and influence the change process? If not, how can you expand opportunities for involvement and influence as a key strategy for driving commitment to the change?
- What tactics can you use to increase conversations between advocates of the change and those who are sitting on the fence?
- Are you seeking people's compliance or their commitment to the change? What will you do to gain people's commitment?

3. **SPONSORSHIP.** A sponsor is a senior leader who has the formal authority to deploy resources (e.g., time, money and people) toward the initiation, implementation and sustainability of a change initiative. An effective change sponsor should:

- Select and align a well-qualified leadership team to lead the change on a day-to-day basis.

- Get commitment and secure buy-in for change by surfacing and addressing concerns and involving those being asked to change in the decision-making process.
- Model the behaviors expected of others, remembering that actions speak louder than words.
- Create incentive by recognizing and reinforcing the behaviors consistent with the change.
- Foster accountability by showing the organization that leadership is serious about change.

ASK THESE QUESTIONS:

- Are the sponsors for change in your organization using the behaviors listed above?
- If your sponsors are not using the behaviors listed above, do they know they are expected to use these behaviors?
- If your sponsors don't know what is expected of them, how will you educate them?

4. **CHANGE LEADERSHIP TEAM.** The change leadership team is the group of leaders with day-to-day responsibility for executing a variety of change leadership strategies to lead people through change and deliver the business outcomes of the change initiative. This team should include people who:

- Have been part of successful change efforts.
- Can allocate the time required.
- Have the respect of their peers.
- Are highly skilled.
- Are willing to speak truth to power.
- Are effective communicators.
- Represent diverse viewpoints, including different areas and levels of the organization as well as advocates, informal leaders and resisters.

It is critical that the change leadership team communicates consistently about the change, regardless of who is communicating.

ASK THESE QUESTIONS:

- Do you have the right people on your day-to-day change leadership team?
- Are the members of your change leadership team speaking with one voice?
- Have you created multiple change leadership teams to effectively carry the change into all areas of the organization?

5. **COMMUNICATION.** The importance of effective communication to the success of a change initiative cannot be underestimated. Effective change communication is:

- Focused on creating dialogue—not one-way communication—with change leaders and those being asked to change.
- Frequent and orchestrated via many different kinds of media—a good rule of thumb is at least seven times and seven different ways.
- Consistent in its message, regardless of who is communicating.
- Delivered by credible, respected sponsors, aligned leadership team members and advocates for the change.

ASK THESE QUESTIONS:

- How effective is the communication regarding the change?
- If less than ideal, how will you improve the effectiveness of the communication?
- Have you surfaced and addressed the questions and concerns of those being asked to change?
- What tactics can you use to increase conversations between advocates of the change and those who are sitting on the fence?

6. **URGENCY.** Urgency explains why the change is needed and how quickly people must change the way they work. If people do not have a sense of urgency regarding the need to change, the inertia of the status quo will likely prove too strong and people will not make the changes you are seeking. The following methods can be used to create a sense of urgency among those being asked to change:

- Bring people face-to-face with the reality of the situation. Share lots of information and involve them in identifying the gap between what is and what could be.

- Provide credible, believable reasons to change, answering the question "What is wrong with the way things are now?" Develop a shared spirit of discontent with the status quo.
- Frame the change in terms of a cause that is motivating.

ASK THESE QUESTIONS:

- Do the people being asked to change see what's wrong with maintaining the status quo?
- Do they have a sense of urgency about the need to change?
- If people's sense of urgency is less than ideal, what will you do to create a stronger case for change and a greater sense of urgency?

7. **VISION.** For those being asked to change, a clear and compelling vision allows them to see themselves succeeding in the picture of the future. Vision should:

- Work with urgency to break the inertia of the status quo.
- Go beyond a slogan and present a clear picture of what the future looks like when the change is successfully implemented.

- Get many people involved in the visioning process so there is ownership beyond the aligned leadership team.
- Allow people to see themselves succeeding in the picture of the future.

ASK THESE QUESTIONS:

- Have the people being asked to change been asked what would get them excited to be part of the post-change organization?
- Can people describe how their future role will be different from—and hopefully better than—their current role?

8. **PLAN.** The change implementation plan is important, but the planning process is even more important. An effective planning process:

- Includes people who are being asked to change, especially resisters who can anticipate what could go wrong.
- Provides enough details for support people on the front line to get going.
- Clarifies priorities.
- Defines the metrics so you'll know if you've been successful.

- Includes pilots using early adopters who are willing to tackle the challenge of making the change work.
- Prepares for the need to have "quick wins" to sway those people who are undecided about whether to support the change.
- Develops the right infrastructure to support the change and ensures that you don't skimp on investments in infrastructure.

ASK THESE QUESTIONS:

- Based on the criteria above, how effective is your planning process?
- If less than ideal, how will you improve the process and the resulting plan?

9. **BUDGET.** No change initiative can be successful without spending money. That being said, it's important to analyze proposed changes from a financial perspective to determine how best to allocate limited resources and ensure a healthy return on investment (ROI). Remember these important points regarding the budget:

- Sponsors control the budget, not the other way around. Ensure that your sponsors clearly buy in to the business case for the change or the budget will overwhelm them at the first sign of trouble with the change.
- Make sure you don't skimp on investments in infrastructure.
- Ensure that you leverage low-cost methods of generating buy-in (e.g., leaders who walk the talk and reinforce desired behaviors; advocates for the change who are in frequent conversations with those who are undecided).

ASK THESE QUESTIONS:

- Have your sponsors committed the budget required to enable the change to succeed?
- What critical levers of change are receiving a smaller budget than necessary?
- Are any areas receiving a larger budget than necessary?

10. **TRAINER.** A change trainer provides learning experiences to ensure that those being asked to change have the skills needed to execute the change and succeed in the future organization. An effective change trainer should be able and willing to:

- Look at a situation and assess the concerns of the people who are being asked to change.
- Comfortably use a variety of change leadership strategies.
- Partner with the people who are being asked to change so that they can voice their concerns, influence the change process and increase their commitment to the change.
- Diagnose the development needs of a team member on a specific goal or task and provide the necessary direction and/or support to meet those needs (i.e., be a situational leader).

ASK THESE QUESTIONS:

- Are you competent and committed to being an effective change leader or coach, using the skills defined above?
- Are you providing job-specific training to give people the skills they need to adopt the change?
- Are you using credible, early adopters of the change to deliver training as a way to increase conversations between advocates and those who are making up their mind about the change?
- What skill barriers are present or can be anticipated in relation to this change? What can you do to overcome these barriers?

11. **INCENTIVE.** Incentive reinforces the desired behaviors and results that enable the change. Many people confuse incentives with monetary rewards. Numerous research studies have shown that well-deserved recognition often goes further toward reinforcing desired behaviors than monetary rewards. Effective incentives:

- Are aligned with the desired behaviors and performance that the change seeks to address.
- Are individualized and available to more than just a handful of people.
- Don't over-incentivize the adoption of change at the expense of people's other important performance goals that are unrelated to the change (e.g., selling a product or service).

ASK THESE QUESTIONS:

- Do you know what motivates each of your team members? If not, how will you find out?
- What creative ideas do you have to recognize people for their hard work, desired behaviors and performance?

12. **PERFORMANCE MANAGEMENT.**
Performance management is the process that sets goals and expectations regarding the behaviors and results that will enable change. The performance management process:

- Includes tracking progress toward the goals and expectations.
- Provides feedback and coaching.
- Formally documents actual results versus desired results.

ASK THESE QUESTIONS:

- Are you clear on how performance will be measured? Are you looking at leading indicators (e.g., people adopting new skills and processes) as well as lagging indicators (e.g., financial performance)? What leading indicators have you defined?
- Do you have a way to measure progress on an ongoing basis, as well as assessing the risks that still need to be addressed?
- Are the people being asked to change clear about what behaviors and results are expected of them and by when?
- Are there processes in place to ensure that those being asked to change are given data and feedback about their performance relative to expectations?
- Are those being asked to change clear about the incentives and consequences for behavior and results that are aligned or misaligned with the change?

13. **ACCOUNTABILITY.** Accountability is the process of following through with people to ensure their behaviors and results are in line with agreed upon goals and expectations. It ensures that leaders are walking the talk by creating consequences when behaviors or results are inconsistent with those that enable change. Accountability is a must for change to have a chance to succeed. Hallmarks of effective accountability are:

- Clearly defined measures of success—goals that are SMART (Specific, Measurable, Attainable, Relevant and Trackable/Time-bound).
- Regular meetings to check progress and plan actions to keep the change on track.
- Two-way accountability—partnering for performance between leader and team member, with each party accountable to the other.
- No favoritism. Everyone is held accountable—senior leaders, managers and the front line. Remember, what leaders do is twice as important as what they say, and what leaders reinforce is three times as important as what they say.

ASK THESE QUESTIONS:

- Are leaders holding themselves and others accountable for adopting the change and embedding it in the culture?
- Which leaders in your organization are the best at holding people accountable for behavior change and performance? What skills and processes do they use?
- How can you replicate these same accountability skills and processes in other areas of your organization?

Good luck with your change initiative! And remember:

*

*Change Can Be Successful Only
When The Usual Characters
In An Organization
Combine Their Unique Talents
And Consistently
Involve Others In
Initiating,
Implementing
And Sustaining
Change*

*

About the Authors

KEN BLANCHARD is an international bestselling author and motivational speaker whose books, including *The One Minute Manager*®, *The One Minute Entrepreneur*™, and *Leading at a Higher Level*, have sold more than eighteen million copies in thirty languages. He lives in San Diego, California.

JOHN BRITT has provided change guidance to a number of large organizations over the last twenty years. He is a partner with Mountjoy and Bressler, LLP, where he continues to provide change leadership and management consulting. John lives in Louisville, Kentucky, and can be reached at jbritt@mountjoybressler.com or +1.270.791.2496.

JUDD HOEKSTRA is one of The Ken Blanchard Companies' experts in leading change and coauthor of its Leading People Through Change program, as well as coauthor of *Leading at a Higher Level*. He also leads high-performing teams for some of Blanchard's strongest client partnerships.

PAT ZIGARMI is a founding associate of The Ken Blanchard Companies, where she currently serves as vice president for business development. She is the coauthor of *Leadership and the One Minute Manager* and *Leading at a Higher Level*.

Services Available

The Ken Blanchard Companies® is a global leader in workplace learning, productivity, performance and leadership effectiveness that is best known for its Situational Leadership® II program—the most widely taught leadership model in the world. Because of its ability to help people excel as self-leaders and as leaders of others, SLII® is embraced by Fortune 500 companies as well as mid- to small-size businesses, governments and educational and nonprofit organizations.

Blanchard® programs—which are based on the evidence that people are the key to accomplishing strategic objectives and driving business results—develop excellence in leadership, teams, customer loyalty, change management and performance improvement. The company's continual research points to best practices for workplace improvement, while its world-class trainers and coaches drive organizational and behavioral change at all levels and help people make the shift from learning to doing.

Leadership experts from The Ken Blanchard Companies® are available for workshops, consulting and keynote addresses on organizational development, workplace performance and business trends.

Global Headquarters
The Ken Blanchard Companies
125 State Place
Escondido, CA 92029
www.kenblanchard.com
+1.800.728.6000 from the United States
+1.760.489.5005 from anywhere

Leading People Through Change

Change is never easy. Roughly 70 percent of change efforts fail or are derailed. Failure of an organizational change can lead to destructive outcomes, such as low productivity and morale, unmet expectations, wasted time and money and increased employee turnover.

Leading People Through Change teaches leaders how to identify and address the typical questions employees raise during a change, as well as how to use the appropriate change leadership strategy and corresponding behaviors to resolve concerns. These strategies are used to address the most common causes of failure in an organization and to address the predictable stages of concern. The model presented in this program can be applied to all types of change efforts, including mergers and acquisitions, business process reengineering, sales force expansion and technology implementations.

Contact The Ken Blanchard Companies® at +1.760.489.5005 to find out how your company can improve the buy-in, commitment and performance of the people who are being asked to change.

Social Networking

Visit Blanchard on YouTube
Watch thought leaders from The Ken Blanchard Companies®
in action. Link and subscribe to Blanchard's channel and
you'll receive updates as new videos are posted.

Join the Blanchard Fan Club on Facebook
Be part of our inner circle and link to Ken Blanchard on
Facebook. Meet other fans of Ken and his books. Access
videos and photos and get invited to special events.

Join Conversations with Ken Blanchard
Blanchard's blog, HowWeLead.org, was created to inspire
positive change. It is a public service site devoted to
leadership topics that connect us all. This site is nonpartisan
and secular, and does not solicit or accept donations. It is a
social network where you will meet people who care deeply
about responsible leadership. And it's a place where Ken
Blanchard would like to hear your opinion.

Keynote Speakers

Blanchard keynote speakers present enduring leadership insights at all types of management-related events, including corporate gatherings and celebrations, association conferences, sales meetings, industry conferences and executive retreats. Our network of speaking professionals is among the best in the world at inspiring audiences to new levels of commitment and enthusiasm.

Blanchard Speaker Topics Include:

- Coaching
- Customer Loyalty
- Employee Engagement
- Leadership
- Motivation and Inspiration
- Organizational Change
- Public Sector Leadership
- Team Building
- Women in Leadership

To book a Blanchard Keynote Speaker for your next event, please call:

United States: +1.800.728.6052
United Kingdom: +44.1483.456300
Canada: +1.800.665.5023
International: +1.760.489.5005

Or visit www.kenblanchard.com/speakers to learn more and to book your speaker today.

Tools for Change

Visit www.kenblanchard.com and click on Tools for Change to learn about workshops, coaching services and leadership programs that will help your organization create lasting behavior changes that have a measurable impact.

Contact Information

United Kingdom
The Ken Blanchard Companies
Gateway Guildford
Power Close
Guildford
Surrey, GU1 1EJ
Tel: + 44 (0) 1483 456300
Fax: + 44 (0) 1483 453157
Email: uk@kenblanchard.com

Global Headquarters
The Ken Blanchard Companies
125 State Place
Escondido, CA 92029 USA
Tel: 800 728 6000 (within the US)
Tel: +1 760 489 5005 (from anywhere)

For a list of our offices worldwide, please visit www.kenblanchard.com